BRING YOUR FRIEND TO CHRIST

Make a Friend, Be a Friend

BRING YOUR FRIEND TO CHRIST

Inspired by The Holy Spirit

Created by Cursillistas

BRING YOUR FRIEND TO CHRIST
Sharon Shymansky Roberts/Tommy Smith
Copyright © 2024

Comments – shroberts164@gmail.com

Images courtesy of Freepik
www.Freepik.com

ISBN: 979-8-218-40188-7

Published by
Truth, Beauty, and Goodness Productions
Columbia, South Carolina

Dedication

This book is dedicated to the thousands of Catholic Cursillistas who have attended their weekends throughout the country and the world. God called you to that weekend, and He gave you a mission. As badly as our world is hurting right now, YOU are the light that will help Him accomplish His goal of bringing the world to Him. Walk boldly in your Fourth Day. You have been Chosen!

TABLE OF CONTENTS

Know Yourself Summary   Deacon Coleman Parks

My First Encounter with Sister Stan   Joan Tucker

Change Me, Then Change the World   Janeth Garcia Hernandez

What's in A Name   Marianne Joy

I Found My Purpose in Cursillo   Judy Clarke

The Prodigal Son Summary   Deacon Robert Pierce

My Prodigal Son   Sharon Shymansky Roberts

Prodigal Son Reflection   Sister Mary Frances Epplin, FSP

The Three Glances of Christ Summary   Deacon Michael Thompson

Saviour and Jesus   Joan Tucker

My Fourth Day   Omar Rivera

The Three Glances Reflection   Sister Mary Frances Epplin, FSP

Introduction

This book came about by the prompting of the Holy Spirit and it is meant to glorify God. It is He who has placed it in your hand, and He who knows what you need to receive from it. Trust in Him, read and enjoy, and find within its pages what He wants you to know and do.

The audience is primarily Catholic Cursillistas, but any Christian is welcome to pick up this book and read it. The Cursillo Movement, Cursillo de Cristiandad, is a laity movement within the Catholic Church that started in Majorca, Spain in the 1940's. It has the same mission that all Christians have – to proclaim the Good News to the world. By proclaiming that news through authentic friendship, we become the hands, feet, and voices that bring the entire world to Christ.

Since the 1940's, Cursillo has spread worldwide, and we imagine there are hundreds of thousands of men and women who have made a Cursillo Weekend and have been charged with changing their environments for Christ. Out of that number, there is likely a low percentage of Cursillistas who have served on at least one Cursillo team. Since you can only attend a Cursillo weekend as a candidate <u>once</u> in your lifetime, that means most Cursillistas never relive a Cursillo weekend. Perhaps you kept your notebook from your weekend; perhaps you've even glanced at it once or twice. But the entire wealth of information imparted to you on that weekend is never lived again.

Much research about the efficacy of corporate training programs has been done, and we believe the same data likely applies to any Christian retreat, even to our beloved Cursillo Weekends. Researchers largely agree that, within one hour of leaving the event, people have forgotten an average of 50% of the information presented. Within 24 hours, 70% has been forgotten and, within the first week after the experience, up to 90%! Lesson learned? If Cursillo was indeed a memorable and life-changing experience for you, join a team now! It is the best way to recapture and revisit that treasure of information.

OR, you can read this book! Albeit, not as good as reliving your weekend as a team member, this book will walk you through the entire weekend of talks in the order they happen. Each chapter begins with a summary of the message of the talk. Each summary is followed by stories written by Cursillistas throughout the state of South Carolina and beyond who are living out their Fourth Day, exemplifying the message found in the summary. The stories will touch your hearts, inspire you, give you confidence to fulfill your Christian mission, and give you new tools to do it! After each summary and story is a short reflection space where you are encouraged to write your reactions and inspirations taken from the writing. We hope you take advantage of that space!

It was such a joy for us to receive these stories from Cursillistas and to have the privilege to put them together into this book for you! We pray it will impact you as much as it has us.

The world needs Christ, and He expects us to help change our world for Him. That is why He called us to Cursillo. By spreading Christ to everyone we know, in every environment where we spend time, we fulfill that mission. Our prayer is that you find in this book the courage to do just that. De Colores!

Tommy Smith and Sharon Shymansky Roberts

Thursday

Where am I on my walk with Jesus?

And So It Begins!
Tommy Smith

What have I gotten myself into? That was the thought I had on a Thursday night in February 2003, as I entered Our Lady of the Lake in Chapin, South Carolina to begin my Cursillo weekend. You may have felt the same or, perhaps, you felt great anticipation. Either way, all of us were beginning something unique and unusual. After the welcoming and typical housekeeping rules, the Rector opened with a story about a farmer and his wife and the purchase of a heating and air conditioning system for their farmhouse. The story continued, introducing the possibility the farmer had been swindled, as the system took a while to arrive. Eventually, it did, only to find it arrived in many boxes without instructions. After a sleepless night of wondering what to do, the farmer was surprised early the next morning when the laborers arrived and began unboxing the system. Miraculously, it all fit together, one box at a time. Slowly it dawned on me this story had a connection to this weekend. The laborers (the team) would be unpacking boxes for us and each would connect to the ones before. Eventually, we would have a complete picture. But of what? With that literary masterpiece and the question it instilled running rampant in my head, we entered into silence. And so, it began.

Many of us did not have the benefit of the Bankruptcy rollos on Thursday night. These talks have been recently added for all Cursillo weekends because they enhance the silent retreat by having the candidates, as well as the team, reflect on where we are in our relationship with God. For those who have not heard them, the point of the stories will still resonate with you. As you remember, Thursday evening, after the Rector's introduction, we entered silence and then heard a reflection on The Prodigal Son. The silence and reflection allowed us to focus on our relationship with God and whether we were moving toward Him or away from Him. More likely we were neutral. Then along came a few stories that helped us enter that question like Alice in Wonderland diving into the rabbit hole.

The banker, John Columbini, and the rich young girl both had their lives devoted to false gods. In a few cases, the stories may have been told with exaggeration, but still drove home the question, "Am I being like them?" The stories invited us to view our past and current lives through the lens of what has been important to us and the worth of living our lives for temporary pleasure, honor, or fame. The silence gave us the space, without distraction, to reflect on the question, " I call myself a Christian, but do I live it?" The Bankruptcy Rollos gave us a foundation to assess if we are putting our lives in the hands of false gods, and the parable of The Prodigal Son said, "I can go back to my Father and He will run to me and welcome me home." WOW!

We did not know what to expect when we came in the door on Thursday evening. Yet, by the end of the evening, in the dead of silence, we began opening our hearts and minds to some fundamental questions about life and where we are going. Are we on the right or wrong path, and where does Jesus fit into all this? We may not have seen it then, but The Holy Spirit was beginning to touch all of us. And, wow, we were in for three very long but glorious days ahead!

Chapter One
Know Yourself

Know Yourself Summary
Deacon Coleman Parks

Your entire Cursillo weekend was all about learning to make God the most important thing in your life. Your first meditation on Thursday night was to help you respond and open yourself up to the Holy Spirit.

Can you imagine what it was like to be an original disciple of Christ? The fears and problems of dealing with tough living conditions? The conflicts between the Jews and the Romans? The conflicts between Jew versus Jew as they struggled to accept this prophet as the Messiah, the son of God? The first disciples certainly had plenty of reasons to worry, but worrying never really helped them, nor does it help us. Does worrying add anything to our lives?

In Matthew 6: 26-34, Jesus said, "Therefore I tell you, do not worry about your life, what you will eat or drink; or about your body, what you will wear. Is not life more than food, and the body more than clothes? Look at the birds of the air; they do not sow or reap or store away in barns, and yet your heavenly Father feeds them. Are you not much more valuable than they? Can any one of you, by worrying, add a single hour to your life?" God's plan is to PROVIDE for ALL our needs. Most of us lose hours of our life worrying and, so often, it's about things that should be left up to God. You must firmly grasp this simple fact: God is perfect; you are NOT!

God has never created anything without a purpose. He has a very special plan for each of us. God has great concern for your welfare and needs, and He brought us into this world to PROVIDE for us. Each of us is unique and different in so many ways, but ALL of us are from God's one design, made in His image and likeness, given dominion over all His creations. We were given not just a mind, but a soul as well. If you want to know the true purpose of your life, start with God, because no one knows you better than your own Creator. So, let's ask Him for answers to these fundamental questions: **Who am I**? **Where am I going**? **What is my life all about**?

The Greek Philosopher Socrates' motto was "Know Thyself." Then Saint Augustine perfected that thought by focusing on God FIRST and then on self, saying, "That I may know Thee, O Lord, and that I may know myself." Also consider Ephesians 1: 11-12. "It is in Christ that we find out who we are and what we are living for," and Colossians 1: 16, "Everything, absolutely everything, got started in Christ and finds its purpose in Him."

It took me a long time to learn that this life is really a preparation for the next life. I learned this from a very young "theologian" when I asked him," What do you think life is all about?" He stared at me for a moment, and then with the most sincere and beautiful smile, he said," It's a test. It's a test, Daddy." From the mouth of my five-year-old son, such wisdom! (Revelations 4:11. "God created everything, and it is for your pleasure that they exist and were created, and the Lord takes pleasure in all of it, just as a father takes pleasure in his child.") This inspired me. If you want to understand how God interacts with us, you must look carefully at the very important relationship between a parent and a child. God is our Father in heaven, just as He is on Earth. Think about that next time you pray the "Our Father."

Having children and trying to be a good mother or father is not always an easy task. Children, like us, are not always good. They fall. We pick them up, forgive them, and try to give them direction. This is exactly what our God does with us and why it is important that we acknowledge God as the Father of every human being, of the entire human family. All are created to be His children. We are intrinsically and intuitively wired to find Him, and you will never find any lasting happiness in this world until you find it in Him!

But fortunately, or unfortunately, we are both blessed and cursed by free will. Ever since God created Adam and Eve, we've struggled with that free will. Want to get to heaven? Learn to manage your free will. The only way to get into heaven is by knowing and loving God. The way to show your love to Him is by surrendering your free will to Him.

Think about this. What if there was a movie made of your life? Would you be able to view all your actions, your ambitions, and your conversations on the screen without embarrassment? Would you want your family or friends or God to view it? Well, don't worry. The Lord has already seen your movie. In fact, He's seen it all, even the ending, yet He still loves you, forgives you, and hopes for you just like a good parent does for his child.

How lucky you were that God brought you to your Cursillo weekend. His Amazing Grace transformed you in a very beautiful way. Prayerfully you relaxed, were joyful, shared that joy, and made new friends with people who love God. They were all around you! Have you ever noticed that little extra joy in people who love God? Matthew 18:20. "Wherever two or more are gathered in My name, there am I in the midst of them." I never really thought about that verse carefully. At first, I thought there had to be two or more *people* because, in a physical sense, that statement would be true under that condition. But what about God, who lives in the Spirit, who Himself promised, "I will be with you till the end of time"? Now I smile when I hear that two or more stuff because, when it's only you, God makes two! And you and God, well, that's always a majority!

If you are honest with yourself, you discovered who you really were that weekend, and not who you wanted people to think you were. You came to truly KNOW THYSELF. Remember, God is like a hopeful parent. He loves you just as you are, but He knows you can do better, be better.

The goal of every Cursillo weekend is to move every participant closer to God by deepening their understanding of how God sees them and how they should see Him. My prayer is that we succeeded in doing just that for you on your weekend!

MY REFLECTION ____

____

____

My First Encounter with Sister Stan
Joan Tucker

As a Cursillista, I am aware that each Mass and Eucharistic Celebration is a miracle of Grace sent to us by God. We can accept this fully or just be a bystander. Our choice. That's how God works. Sometimes He even places people in our paths whom we can choose to ignore or choose to embrace. That's how it was with Sister Stan.

My journey began one Sunday in 2014. Our parish priest had invited one of his relatives, Revered Sister Stan Mumuni, to speak to our congregation about her ministry in West Africa. Although small in stature, she was a powerful speaker, and her message was profoundly impactful. She told us of the appalling practice that takes place in many of the villages in Northern Ghana. There the villagers live in small communities inside a house made of mud with a grass roof. They have no running water or electricity.

They hold tightly to their ancient tribal beliefs that any child born with a deformity, any child who doesn't walk or talk by the age of three, any child who is a twin, or any child born where the mother dies during childbirth is a vessel for an evil spirit who entered the child while still in the womb. Once that child is identified as a "Spirit Child," the family must hire a concoction man to gather poisonous herbs and feed them to the child to kill both the child and the spirit within.

I was totally awestruck hearing her message about the orphanage she had started to rescue and care for these children and by her plea for financial assistance. The Holy Spirit stirred in my heart and, by the time Mass was over, I had made up my mind that I could do so much more than write a check to help Sister and her children. I approached Sister in the Narthex and told her I was a retired nurse. I asked if I could be of any help to her and her children. She had at this point rescued 32 children from death. She was happy to accept!

That was it! I just blurted it out, and that sealed my commitment to her. Now I just had to break it to my husband that I had offered to go to Ghana for a couple of months. Surprisingly, he was immediately and unconditionally supportive of my plans. I'm sure the Holy Spirit touched his heart as well.

By January of 2015, I was boarding my first of many flights to Ghana. When there, I helped examine the children and take those who needed further care to local hospitals. I arranged and distributed the seizure medication to those with epilepsy. I also trained one of the local hires on how to treat wounds and administer the medication as needed.

During my early times in Ghana, I was able to arrange for Abraham, a young boy with hydrocephalus, to receive a groundbreaking procedure in Uganda that drained the fluid and saved his life thanks to CURE UGANDA and God's grace. After a lengthy process, I was also able to procure care at Shriners Children's Hospital for Saviour, a child with cerebral palsy. I made at least seven trips to and from Nazareth Home for God's Children over the next few years, until I was grounded by the Covid pandemic. By God's grace, I have resumed those trips.

All of what I just related to you was not something I was able to accomplish by myself. Remember, Christ and I are an overwhelming majority! To quote St. Therese of Lisieux, "Christ has no body now on earth but yours. No hands, no feet on earth but yours. Yours are the eyes through which Christ looks his compassion on this world. Yours are the feet with which he goes about doing good. Yours are the hands with which he is to bless us now."

MY REFLECTION ____

____

____

Change Me, Then Change the World
Janeth García Hernandez

I am from Veracruz, Mexico, and I am 33 years old. I lived my Cursillo from October 19 to 22, 2019. I have been given the opportunity to share my 4th day and how I am living it. I do it with a lot of faith, perseverance, and love. It is not easy because the enemy is very evil, but it is not impossible because, for God, nothing is impossible.

Now, I am working first with myself. I try to be a good example for others. I do that through how I have changed my life. It is not perfect because only God is perfect, but I do the best I can although I need to learn more. I can fight my own battles because, when I went to Cursillo, I met God - the only one who loves me as I am - and I discovered that He is everything in my life. He has been so good to me. That's why I want to thank Him by fulfilling his mandates, and I go little by little without stopping. I try to help in everything I can in the parish where I attend; I go to my friendship meetings, Ultreyas, School of Leaders, to masses to continue persevering. If I stop doing it, it will distract me and that's why I don't stop, because I don't want to lose what the Lord has given me.

I was a person who did not value herself; I feared loneliness and wanted to find love in someone. I lived a lot of abuse as a child by my father, but God sent me an Angel for a mom. She did what she could to protect me and my two brothers. Maybe it was not much, because she was also beaten by my dad, but for me, it was more than enough. I left home at 18 with someone who convinced me that it was time. One can get carried away by others when you do not believe you can make your own decisions. So, I left, not because I wanted to or even because I liked the person. I believed that what happened in my life then was what was coming to me, just as what happened to my mother. I also suffered abuse and beatings when I was pregnant, but I never asked for help from my mother out of sorrow, and I endured it on my own. I told myself that I deserved it for not listening to Mom, but I was rebellious and had no fear of God.

By the grace of God, He took that person away from my life back to his country because I alone could not have done it. After four years of abuse, I was alone with my 3-year-old daughter, but life taught me I had to get ahead. Due to my work, I neglected my daughter, and I cried because I missed her. A person assured me that it was for the best, and I convinced myself that it was the best to give my daughter everything that I did not have. It got to a point where my daughter stopped calling me Mom and called me by my name. My sister took care of her and she was her mother, but God opened my eyes and made me realize what was happening. From there on, I began to think differently about what the most important thing in life was. Love is, and so I vowed to take better care of my daughter.

I met someone else, and I fell back into the trap. What a fool I was, but I now know it was because I wanted to feel true love and to be treated better. For me, it was a dream that I did not deserve until everything changed. For four years of my life, it was like this. I had a baby but the father never wanted to live with me or take responsibility. I felt guilty for I allowed it and made bad decisions, and I felt that he was worth more than me. It was so bad that I fell into depression, about to commit suicide, but I never managed to do it. I had two children and I thought, what would happen to them? At that time, I knew a little about God, and He put me before an amazing woman, a friend who helped me and gave me the time to talk and stop before trying to commit suicide. I saw that my daughter was imitating me and she was only six years old. Thank God I did not do it, and I came out stronger and sought help when needed.

Now I know more about God. Many more things continued to happen. I found myself going from one place to another looking for a better opportunity without luck, but I searched and, little by little, I found the Way to become a strong and independent woman. However, as time passed, loneliness knocked at my door again, and men approached me to offer me love. I trusted and only received hurt. My problem was I did not know my courage, and I did not love myself. I sometimes denied God. I was not patient, had nothing, and I fell apart.

Four years ago, I learned about the Cursillo and there I began to make a real-life change. The problem was me and money. It seemed I could not have something of my own. But God gave me the opportunity through my mom and people who supported me with money. I could pay them little by little because only then could I do it, and I really thanked them. I became more responsible and saw that I could only realize my dreams if I changed and learned to wait. Then, I began to fight my own battle of loneliness and I won. I never lost hope of someday finding someone who would love me, protect me, and respect my children, but no longer was it my main priority. I learned to be patient. I knew myself more, but there were still temptations. Little by little, I was moving them away, and my life changed for the better. It was with the love of God, and my growing love for Him, that I began trying to live the example of our Lord Jesus Christ.

A year ago, I met that person. God gave me so many signs that I discovered them and now he is my husband. I am married by the church, and I have a beautiful baby of five months, even though I said I did not want more children. Now there are three. I am the first in my family to be married in the Church, and I am happy because I live in Grace with the Lord, and I do not want to lose it. We have opened the door to God so that my children have better opportunities and a better example. My husband is also a Cursillista, and he used to go alone to the Blessed Sacrament because he is a lector. Now my children and I accompany him. We are a big happy family.

A sister, called Martha, told me that if you want to find love, a person should love God first, and that was the truth, and it was how I found love. I will continue to love and serve Him until he calls me on my Fifth day. De Colores!

MY REFLECTION ____

____

____

What's in a Name?
Marianne Joy

One day recently, I got to thinking about the importance of

names and why God chose to change the names of certain figures in biblical history. **There are names given by humans and names given by God.** *"We know from sacred Scripture how seriously God took names. He famously changed the names of Abram to Abraham, Sarai to Sarah, Jacob to Israel and Simon to Peter. He commanded Zechariah to name his son John, to incarnate God's graciousness, and Joseph to name Mary's Son, Jesus, to enflesh and effectuate God's salvation... To give someone a name, as we see from the beginning, is a sacred act, an act that participates in God's creative plan, a solemn responsibility that should be carried out with prayer and joyful seriousness..."* https://www.catholicculture.org/culture/library/view.cfm?recnum=9588

    Each change of name had important significance in relation to God's plan. *"For the average student of the Bible, who starts his or her study '"in the beginning" with the book of Genesis, it doesn't take long to realize that names play a significant role throughout sacred Scripture. They reveal a certain characteristic or mark an event, in the lives of people and the history of places. Names are sometimes changed as well... Why is that? Why does God change people's names? The short answer to that question is that a name change signifies a new call in life. It is symbolic of a new identity.*

" https://www.simplycatholic.com/changing-names

My last name makes me happy. Which is why I picked it! Long story short, before my Cursillo weekend, my life was very different than what it is now. I went to church once a week, but that was the end of it. I was not living my faith. I was miserable inside. I worked with my (now ex) husband who was a successful businessman. On the outside, it looked like I had it all. But when I answered the phone, he didn't even want me to use my own name. I had to pretend that my name was Melissa. "This is business," I was told. By the time our non-sacramental marriage ended; I had no idea what my identity was.

After my Cursillo weekend, everything changed. I realized the truth in the Scripture, ***"What good will it do a person if he gains the whole world, but forfeits his soul? Or what will a person give in exchange for his soul?" (Matthew 16:26)*** Everything changed. I changed. And I decided to legally change my last name to Joy because I felt different inside. I wanted a name that reflected the person I wanted to be. Well, I'm not claiming to have an elaborate mission, but I do know that God has a plan for each one of us and, as Catholics, we all must strive to fulfill His plan for our lives. And I wanted to share my new-found Joy with the whole world.

Most people don't go to the extreme of changing their last names like I did, but we can change our attitudes. This will influence our environments, especially when people discover that our Joy is coming from Christ shining within us. This Joy is what draws people to us Cursillistas. And this gives us the opportunity to tell them how they can find this Joy for themselves. Be the Joy! De Colores!

MY REFLECTION ____

____

____

I Found My Purpose in Cursillo
Judy Clarke

In January of 2022, as I was sitting in church waiting for mass to begin, Dr. Tim Joseph spoke to our parish about the Cursillo movement. The speech intrigued me and sounded somewhat familiar.

My husband had passed away in October 2021, and I was

struggling with the question of my usefulness. I was 82 years old; my sons were 60 and 61 years old, and I felt that I was ready to meet my Lord. To be honest, I wasn't depressed, I just had no purpose.

Cursillo sounded interesting. Maybe I could try a new adventure. The bulletin listed Sharon Roberts' name and phone number, so I gave her a call. She was kind, welcoming, and full of information. We met for coffee and she invited me to participate in the Thursday morning Cursillo grouping. It was an inspiring experience, and it convinced me to attend the weekend. That was the beginning of my extraordinary spiritual journey.

I was speaking to my brother, John, who lives in Virginia about my decision to attend a Cursillo weekend. He told me that he and my sister-in-law had made their Cursillo in 1980 in Virginia. He had never really spoken about the experience to me, but I recall him going to a men's meeting at the church every Saturday morning. That was his grouping. He also said that they had been on team, but at the time that really had no meaning to me. He wanted to know where I was going to attend the weekend. I had no idea except that it was in Columbia.

My Cursillo #76 was the most profound experience of my life. During the weekend I experienced the power of the Holy Spirit and the enormous Grace of God. A warm glow filled my heart, and I had an inner peace that I had never experienced before in my life. I was so overwhelmed, I wept. The weekend taught me to recognize the guidance of the Holy Spirit, to feel His comfort, and to learn His purpose in my life. It was life changing.

I realized that my life should be centered on Christ and, if I focus on Him and His word, I will have a close relationship with Him. I began talking to Jesus, one-on-one. I reminded myself to talk to Him first, before I did anything, and I slowly learned how to develop a meaningful prayer life. I learned a lot about myself... some good and some not so good.

I met many faith-filled women on the weekend and was able to make some wonderful new friends. These spirit-filled women joined me on my spiritual journey. That bond of faith and friendship remains strong, encouraging, and loving.

Our Lord also showed me how deeply my brother and sister-in law love me. My brother contacted Precious Blood Church to inquire as to the site of the weekend. He then contacted Sharon, my sponsor. Both my brother, my sister-in-law and several of their friends, whom I knew were Cursillistas, wrote me palancas and, when I exited the door into the closing, my brother and sister-in-law were seated in the front row waiting to greet me. As I am writing this, I am weeping in gratitude.

In conclusion, I now know that God has a journey planned just for me. I am still needed. He is counting on me as much as I count on Him. My journey has just begun. He has given me a purpose. De Colores !

MY REFLECTION ____

____

____

Chapter Two
Prodigal Son

The Prodigal Son
Summary Deacon Robert Pierce

The Parable of the Prodigal Son. This is one of the most distinctive parables of Jesus. I checked the definition of the word "prodigal" and it said, "characterized by profuse or wasteful expenditure; lavish." This is why this parable has also been referred to as the Parable of the Prodigal Father, because while the younger son was wasteful with his money, the father was lavish with his mercy and love.

Recall why Jesus told this parable. Tax collectors and sinners were drawing near to listen to Jesus, but the Pharisees and scribes complained saying, "This man welcomes sinners and eats with them." The younger son definitely represents those sinners, which means the younger son could be any one of us as we have all walked away from the Father at one time or another.

Eventually, the younger son hits rock bottom, but he was already spiritually poor before he ever left home. It is just that now, everyone else can see it, too. He can't hide behind appearances. But, maybe more important is the question of how far have we fallen? How far have we wandered from the Father? Are we able to see ourselves in the younger son?

The older son could be anyone acting as a Pharisee, who is a self-righteous, law-abiding person who knows God only through the law. Jesus is challenging those listening to stop judging <u>others</u> and, instead, examine their own hearts. Learn to see through the eyes of the Father. "Your father has killed the fatted calf, because he has your brother back safe and sound." The servant explains why there is a celebration, but the older son's gaze is on himself.

How prone are **<u>we</u>** to judge and compare ourselves to others?

The Pharisees want to make this discussion about the sinfulness of those with whom Jesus eats (the actions of the younger son). At the end of the parable, Jesus makes the discussion about their hearts (the attitude of the older son). "Listen! For all these years I have been working like a slave for you, and I have never disobeyed your command." How that must have grieved the father. Sonship is more than that. The older son reveals that his heart is not like the father's any more than the younger son's. The most valuable thing either son had was the love of their father, but neither seemed to recognize it.

Ironically, at this point in the story, despite his years of obeying his father's rules, the older son is not part of the celebration. Are we like that? We think we are righteous, but we are stubbornly or selfishly remaining outside of where the father really wants us to be. We are not united to Him and His household. Are we able to see ourselves in the older son?

Now we get to the heart of the matter. The love of the father dominates center stage, as it should. "Filled with compassion." Now it overflows. "He RAN to him, EMBRACED him, and KISSED him." He cannot contain himself. This son of his heart is back. It doesn't matter how dirty and smelly he is. That can be fixed. He is irreplaceable. You are irreplaceable. These are the actions of someone who didn't just notice his son at a distance, but who was waiting and praying for his return. "I've been worried sick about you."

"Bring the finest robe! Put a ring on his finger (the ring signifying that he is family)! Kill the fatted calf! Let us celebrate!

"Wait! I am no longer worthy to be called your son!"

OK?!? But you are my son. Nothing can change that. Ah! The embrace of the father. The younger son finally realizes that there is nothing better in the world than the embrace of the father. If we could get a glimpse of our dignity before our Father, our hearts would melt.

The parable quickly moves from the embrace to the celebration. "But we had to celebrate and rejoice." God, in His nature as love, must celebrate and rejoice at the return of one of those He loves. Our religion is not to do x, y, and z and then God will love you and want to bless you. The Gospel is concerned with the redemption and salvation of souls. It is concerned with the embrace and celebration.

I think this is a major point of contention for the older son. Here I am trying to follow your laws, and the disobedient one is feasting and celebrating. The scribes and Pharisees are not complaining that Jesus is calling sinners to repent. The older son is complaining because by celebrating the finding of what was lost, it seems the father is placing the wayward one on the same level as the obedient one. Outrageous! The father is acting as though the younger son's sins did not happen. Exactly!

There is a story of a priest to whom a woman came saying that Jesus had been talking to her. The priest was highly skeptical but was still gentle with her. The priest said, "OK. The next time Jesus comes to you, ask Him what sins I mentioned in my last confession." The next week, the priest saw the woman and he asked, "So what did Jesus say?" The woman replied, "He said, 'I don't remember.'" The sin is forgotten and, like the younger son, we are restored to full membership in the family. That is cause for celebration.

Awaken to the glory you have as God's child. Answer the invitation to be part of the celebration and unite in the deepest ways to the Father. A good step in the right direction is to recognize your sin and strive to remove any obstacles that exist between you and the Father. That is the purpose of the Sacrament of Reconciliation. The Father's desire is for us to experience His embrace. What we need is a willingness to return.

There is a two-fold dynamic to the entire Cursillo weekend, and it aligns perfectly with this parable. The Cursillo weekend is a weekend of embracing and celebration. First comes the embrace of God, of Mother Church, of the Christian community. Then, aware of our identity and dignity, comes the celebration. Cursillo is literally a short course in Christianity – it prepares us for that same two-fold movement throughout our lives – embrace and celebration. Let us begin anew to open ourselves to the embrace so that we can also join the celebration.

MY REFLECTION _______________________________________

____

____

My Prodigal Son (My story)
Sharon Shymansky Roberts

Remember the parable in Luke 15:11-32 of the prodigal son? That story has always bothered me. Why did the father give the son his portion of the inheritance, when it should pass to both sons upon his death? Why did the youngest son even ask for it? How did that make his father feel? And what about the brother, the oldest son? While I don't justify his rage when he returns from working in the fields and sees the party going on and the fatted calf killed, I can see his point. And finally, the father welcomes his wayward son home lavishly and joyously, even though he is aware his son has squandered the inheritance. On the surface, it all seems a little unfair...until you live it. I had a prodigal son experience, and once I lived it, I fully understood the depths of a parent's joy at having a son return. I also now realize that the prodigal son story is our story, as all of us leave our Father from time to time and become lost. Yet, He is always there to joyously welcome us home when we return with humble hearts. And our heavenly inheritance is waiting for us when we do.

I had been a widow for just two weeks. I still spent most moments of every day crying, wondering if the ache in my heart would ever heal. I drove on autopilot each day to and from work and rotely fixed meals for myself and my nineteen-year-old son, Ryan, when he was home. I still hadn't slept in the bed I had shared with David for 26 years. It was too lonely. So, who could blame Ryan, who was grieving in his own way, for going out nearly every night after work? Who could fault him for staying out way past his midnight curfew? He had watched his father battle cancer every day for over two years. Now he had lost him, and his mother didn't seem to be there for him either.

But I *was* there. I was there every night, wide awake, silently praying that my son would come home safely. Silently begging God to keep him safe. I had just lost one love. "Please God, don't let me lose a second." When the door would open around 2 or 3 am, I would say a prayer of thanks and finally fall asleep.

Gradually, I began to snap out of my overwhelming grief and turned my attention immediately to Ryan, whose late-night habits were continuing. One Saturday, I waited in the breakfast nook for him to wake up. It was long past noon when his growling stomach led him in my direction.

"I'm glad you're finally awake, son. Grab some food and come sit here with me, please. We need to talk."

"Ok." He fixed a sandwich, grabbed some milk, and sat down across from me.

"Ryan, I know that we haven't had much opportunity to be there for each other these past few weeks, and I'm sorry. The past 2 ½ years, with your father being so sick, and then losing him, have really taken a toll on me, but I am getting better, getting stronger. I know you've been grieving too, but what I don't know is why you've decided that our house rules no longer apply to you. Nothing has changed in that department. Even though your dad isn't here, the rules we set still are. You know you have a midnight curfew, don't you?"

"Yes, ma'am."

"Well, you certainly haven't been honoring it, and that has to stop. I lie awake every night until you come home, worrying that something has happened. That just isn't fair to me. Yes, you lost your father, but I lost my husband and my best friend. We had known each other for almost 30 years. I know I haven't been there to help you with your grieving, but I'm here now, so please talk to me. Let me help. Tell me why you aren't following the rules. What's going on in your head and in your life?"

"Nothing. I'm ok."

"You aren't. You have never been blatantly disobedient before. What's going on? Please talk to me."

"I don't have anything to say."

"Nothing? Really? No explanation for why you are staying out late? No apology for causing me to worry?"

"No."

"Okay. Then hear this. I love you. You are my son and nothing is more precious to me than you and your brothers, especially now. But rules are rules. You have a midnight curfew, and I expect you to honor it. I cannot continue to worry like this on top of the heartbreak I am trying to live through. Do you understand?"

"Yes."

"Then here's what must happen. If you cannot abide by the curfew, if you come in past midnight tonight, then I will have no alternative but to ask you to pack your things and leave. It's a simple request. Bring your friends here if you want. They are welcome to stay. But you must be home by midnight. Can you do that?"

"Yes."

"Great. Then we have an agreement. Thank you. Do you have plans for today?"

"Yeah. Dougie and I and some of the guys are going to the park."

"Oh, I thought you and Dougie might want to take out the jet skis. It's warm out there."

"No, Mom. We're just gonna play some ball at the park."

"Ok. Just remember our agreement. Should I fix dinner for you? Or we could go out and eat?"

"Nope. I'll grab something up the road."

"Ok, then. Call me if you need me. I'll be waiting up for you."

I did. I was in the living room, a single light on, waiting for my son to do as he had agreed. At 2 a.m., I dragged myself to bed in my own bedroom, in the bed David and I had shared, hoping that being there would give me the strength to do what I needed to do later that day. Around 3 a.m. I heard the door open. Shortly after, I finally slept, exhausted from worrying and praying.

The next day, Sunday, I went to early mass. When I returned home, I fixed breakfast for us both and waited. Surprisingly, I didn't have long to wait. I suspect Ryan's sleep had been troubled as well, knowing what was to come. He walked zombie-like into the kitchen, where I sat at the breakfast nook.

"Good morning, Ryan. There's breakfast on the kitchen counter. Please bring it here so we can talk. While he was fixing his plate, I turned to gaze out the bay window at the Wicomico River gently lapping at our private beach. It was peaceful today, belying the turmoil erupting in my heart and head. I had given Ryan an ultimatum, and now, unless he could say something to appease my heart, I was about to ask my youngest son to leave his home, perhaps forever. How could I be doing this to him when he was also grieving? My head said there must be consequences to our actions. It was my job to make sure he understood that, or life from this point out would be very difficult for him. He had to go. My heart said that he was my youngest, the one son who had been here every day of those 26 months watching his father suffer. He was hurting, and I needed to help fix it; he should stay. God said nothing, at least nothing I could hear through my pain.

Ryan brought his breakfast to the table, silently eating it. "Please God," I prayed, "give me the courage and the wisdom I need." I took a shaky breath. "Ryan, correct me if I am wrong, but I thought at the end of our talk yesterday that you agreed to abide by the midnight curfew. Am I right or wrong?"

"Right."

"But you didn't. I stayed up until after 2 waiting in the living room for you. Then I lay awake in my bed until 3 a.m. when you came in. What happened to make you go back on your word?"

"Nothing."

"Do you remember what I said I would have to do if you couldn't follow our rules?"

"Yes ma'am."

"Do you have anything to say?"

"No, ma'am."

"Well, then, Ryan, I love you. I have been praying it didn't come to this, but you have made a choice. I think you need to go pack now."

"Yes, ma'am." He left the table without even a backward glance in my direction. And for the second time in less than a month, my heart broke. Fifteen minutes later, I heard the front door close, and the enormity of what I had just done threatened to suffocate me. I began praying immediately. "Please, Jesus and Mary, look out for my son.

Protect him, keep him safe from harm. Bring him home to me."

The first phone call I made was to my husband's best friend, Sam Graves. Both David and Sam had served on the county police force together. Sam had been a godsend throughout David's illness, the funeral, and the aftermath. I knew I could count on him. I filled him in on what I had done, and I begged him to have the guys look out for Ryan. I gave him Ryan's tag # and a description of the car.

Then the waiting began.

MY REFLECTION ________________________________

____

____

A Son's Fall and Rise to Happiness
Ryan Shymansky (His story)

I had just had my universe turned upside down. My world, my hero, and most of all, my father, had died. I was the ultimate daddy's boy. I did anything and everything I could to be able to spend time with him and learn everything I could from him. The day he died was the worst day of my life. I wasn't even there. I had spent the night with a friend, and that evening Mom had called. She told me that Aunt Sherrie, who was a nurse, had been over and said something about Dad's fingernails turning blue. Mom told me we'd only have him with us about another 12 hours. She wanted me to come home, but she said the decision was mine. I decided to stay at my friend's house. I spent the entire night crying for the dad I was about to lose. Early the next morning, my brother called to tell me to come home. Mom needed us all around her. I knew what that meant. He had died, and I hadn't been there. I literally went insane and was fully enraged with anger and hate, a terrible combination for a 19-year-old.

After he died, I went downhill fast and was too stubborn to let anyone know what was going on inside my head or, God forbid, ask me if I wanted to talk about it. Mom tried, but I just bottled it all up inside as I had for the entire time he had been sick. When Mom had told me that first day that he had cancer, I didn't even know what cancer was. I even asked her, "Is he going to die from this?" I knew all that time I watched as he struggled to beat this, that one day I was going to explode and lose control of whatever little bit of myself I had left.

The day came and all the emotions finally just overflowed; I lost complete control of everything. I started drinking way more than I ever had. I started doing drugs to cope with watching my father die. I started lying to Mom and doing anything and everything I had never done before. I had truly become someone I had never been or ever wanted to be, and no one wanted to be around me except for the group of "friends" I had made. I started going out to friends' houses and going to parties and staying out all night drinking and partying it up the best I could. I had no remorse. I didn't care who I hurt, not even my own family. I didn't even care about me. Of course, living at home with Mom had meant having rules but, at that point rules meant nothing to me either.

Eventually, my mom had enough. I wouldn't talk to her, wouldn't open up about what I was doing or how I was feeling. She finally gave me an option to follow the rules or get out. At that point, the easiest decision for me was to roll out, be on my own, live with friends, and party 24/7. I'd have the greatest time ever, so I grabbed clothes and rolled out, not looking back one time. I had not one bit of remorse and never gave a thought to what my leaving would do to my mom.

I ended up sleeping in my car for two nights in the Outback parking lot because I had nowhere to sleep. Eventually, I got a hotel room at a Master Suites. So, of course, I invited all my friends and their friends and so on. Before I knew it, we were having a party every night. Then came the night I was awakened by a loud banging on my door, and I knew instantly it wasn't one of my "friends" knocking.

I stumbled to the door while walking gingerly over people still passed out on the floor from last night's party. At the door stood Mr. Sam Graves, a deputy sheriff like my dad had been, and my father's long-time best friend. He was and still is the second greatest man and role model in my life.

I stepped outside. He informed me that he knew what was going on, who was inside my room, what was inside my room, and, if he wanted to, he could order a search warrant and walk on in. He didn't. Instead, he proceeded to talk to me like a father. He told me about my mom's phone call to him, and how she had begged him to look out for me, keep a watch over me and keep me safe. He said she was scared to death and didn't know if I was alive or dead. He told me how worried he was about me too and how I had disappointed him. He said that he expected so much more out of me than what I had become and that my father would never have wanted me to turn out like this. That speech he gave started to wake me up and kind of bring me out of my coma. I started opening my eyes for the first time in a long time to what I was doing to myself and to the people who loved me. I started feeling remorse and regret, and I started grieving for the loss of my dad, rather than burying those feelings beneath alcohol and drugs. I began, slowly, to make my way back to who I was.

During all this I had made a solid friend who was kind of going through the same thing I was, except she had lost her father the year before, so she was trying to help me get through what she had already experienced. She wasn't very happy with how I was handling it, but she didn't leave me. She stayed, and we became very close. She convinced me to go home. I did.

The day I showed up at the house, my mom came to meet me. I asked her if I could come home. She merely asked if I thought I could live with the rules. When I told her I could, she just cried and hugged me until I thought I was going to break. I was so frail from the drugs and not eating well. I truly thought I might pass out! I sincerely apologized and, from then on, it was my aim in life to get back my smile and my mom's.

I completely changed everything I did, including who I went around with. I stopped doing drugs, though it took some help. I'm sad to say I kept drinking, but nowhere near what I had before, and I started trying to rebuild my relationship with my mother. I didn't want her to have to worry anymore about me going down that bad road.

As luck would have it, as I was trying to rebuild myself, the woman of my dreams and my best friend had our first child, a baby boy we named Kyle. The news of the pregnancy and the birth of my son was my salvation. After all, I had been blessed with an amazing father, and Kyle deserved the same! I had a mission – to be as good to Kyle and his mom as my dad had been to us and my mom.

I have been faithfully and joyously married to my best friend for almost 22 years now. I am the man I wanted to be, the father I wanted to be, and the husband my wife needs me to be. We have added two daughters, first Lily and then Maddie, to our now complete family. I am the proudest father in the universe and the happiest and luckiest husband in the world, because I not only got to marry my best friend, but one of my saviors. I'm also one of the three luckiest sons in the world because I have a mother who believes in unconditional love. She is amazing and forgiving and always full of understanding. I am truly a blessed man!

When I heard someone enter the front door, I naturally headed that way. I stopped at the sight of him. He was haggard and emaciated, but he was home, and by the look on his face, I knew he wanted to stay.

My heart was threatening to leap out of my chest; breathing was getting harder by the second. I held out my arms and he came to me. That's when I knew the intense joy of the prodigal son's father. There is nothing that can compare to the emotion of having a son lost, and then having him return to you safely. I'm sure Ryan's brothers, like the brother in the prodigal son story, did not understand, but they are both fathers now, and one day, I pray, they will. In the meantime, by the Grace of God, my son was home.

MY REFLECTION ____

____

____

The Prodigal Son
Sister Mary Frances Epplin

I'm sure you are familiar with the Gospel account (*Luke 15:11-32)*. If Jesus told the parable today, perhaps it would sound like this:

A man had two sons. The younger said to his father, "Dad, I want my share of your estate _right now_." Saddened, the father liquidated his assets and divided them. A few days later, the young man packed his bags and booked a cruise. Arriving in a distant land, he wasted everything on wild living. He was broke. Then famine struck the region and he was hurt. He got a job with one of the locals, slopping the pigs. He was so hungry—he would have eaten the corncobs.

That brought him to his senses. "What am I doing? Back home, our staff sits down to three squares a day. Why am I here starving to death? I'm going back home and say, 'Father, I've done wrong against God and against you. I don't deserve to be called your son. Take me on as a hired hand.'" He stood up and dashed off. His father, meanwhile, who had been scanning the horizon each day from the dock, saw him hobbling along. Heart pounding, he ran out, embraced him and kissed him. The son started his speech. "Father, I've sinned against God. I've sinned before you. I don't deserve to be called your…"

But the father wasn't listening. He was sending off text messages to the manager: "Quick! Pick out a nice sports jacket, the family ring, and new Birkenstocks. Have some steaks delivered and grill them."

He started shouting, "We're going to have a feast! My son is here—given up for dead—and now he's here alive! He was lost and is now found!" They threw this huge party.

Now the older son was working out. He arrived home and heard the music and dancing. Calling over one of the lawn crew, he asked, *"What's going on ?"*

The servant said, "Your brother's home. Your father has ordered a feast—a big Bar-B-Q! Because he's home safe and sound."

The older brother stomped off and refused to join in. His father went out and tried to reason with him, but he turned away, muttering, "*This ain't fair*. Look how long I've worked with you… *I* never gave you no grief. Did you ever throw a party for me and *my friends?* Here this <u>son *of yours*</u> spends all your hard-earned cash on loose living, shows up now, and you go all out with this *humongous* homecoming!"

"Son, you don't understand," the father assured him. "You're with me all the time, and all I *have* is yours. But this time, we had to celebrate. Your brother was dead, and he's alive! He was lost, and he's found!"

Let's look more closely at the parable. A young man is tired of living with his family and burns to venture out on his own. Tragedy strikes. As a destitute outsider, he realizes that his *do-as-you-please* lifestyle was totally self-destructive.

The story says <u>he came to himself</u>. He suddenly knew who he was…<u>not</u> the young *know-it-all* who defied his parents and religious traditions. He recognized himself as a sinner who had squandered everything, even his own self-respect. The young man had been forced to <u>reflect on his situation</u>, his father's pain, and the misery of separation from his family.

Now he had two choices. He could give up, "My father will never forgive me. My family has certainly disowned me. I'm too ashamed to face them…" Or he could remember his <u>father's loving ways</u> and the joyful family celebrations. It was that <u>memory</u> that saved him and gave him hope.

Now the story takes another twist. The father meanwhile is longing for his child's return. He rushes out to meet his son, embraces him, and kisses him. He enfolds his son in his love, freely and unconditionally.

The elder son's part in the parable shows that—while we can sin by focusing totally on ourselves and neglecting God, resulting in misery and destruction, like the younger son—<u>arrogance,</u> that is, looking <u>down</u> on others <u>is also sin</u>.

My heart still aches when I remember a similar situation: Once, a friend (labeled Ugly Betty by some of our classmates) asked me to spend a day at the park with her. I made the excuse that I was too busy. Apparently, she roamed around the shopping mall alone all afternoon, and then passed by the ice cream shop where she saw me laughing and chatting with some of my other friends. She turned away red-faced. I made an awkward attempt to run after her, "Oh, <u>there you are</u>… uh…Do you like ice cream?" The exuberance in that room fizzled. All my inner insecurities were rubbed raw. She left, letting the door slam. I felt completely unraveled. With my thoughtlessness, I had effectively disowned her.

As we reflect on each of these personalities: the tattered younger child clinging to the one who is faithful and loving, the distant elder child, and the aging half-blind Jewish patriarch, we may find that we are looking into a mirror. God asks us to change our hearts and seek conversion. Each of the figures speaks to us of some aspect of our personal journey through life. Which person in the story are <u>you</u>?

I am the prodigal child. Many times, due to sinful attitudes and addictive habits, we may find ourselves homesick. Sin seduces us to satisfy our senses; and brings emptiness, stress, and tension. Strategies of defense—to avoid being ignored, put down, blamed, "un-friend-ed" sink in. But in doing so, I move farther away from my father's house and choose to dwell in a "distant country." As each crisis invades my fragile life, I feel compelled to return home. I long for the Father's mercy and forgiveness. I <u>need</u> God's loving embrace. Kneeling before the Father, I rest my head against God's chest, and listen to the heartbeat of love that surrounds me.

I am the elder son. I am the elder daughter. Even when we are faithful in our daily duty, we may start to hear other voices. Loud, disturbing voices <u>comparing</u> our lives with others: <u>ranking</u> who is more or less intelligent, more or less attractive, more or less favored.
Maybe they are the voices of our relatives, colleagues, advertising, or media. But without realizing it, these voices begin to dominate life. These tempt and distract us, "Get out and prove you're worth something." "Add more friends to your Facebook or Twitter." "Look out for **#1**." Voices tempt us. We need ***metanoia***, conversion—turning from ourselves to God.

I am called to be the welcoming parent: Let's study the masterpiece again. The loving Father is saying, "You are my beloved child. On you, my favor rests." Whether we have been the <u>elder</u> son/daughter or the <u>younger</u> son/daughter, we are called to reveal the <u>tenderness of God</u>. Every time we heal another's offenses, seek reconciliation, share our possessions, foster the spirit of community, and celebrate the gifts others have received; we are the compassionate father.

Some years ago, Christian songwriter Amy Grant penned these touching lyrics:

> **I may not be every mother's dream for her little girl.**
> **And my face may not grace the mind of everyone in the world.**
> **But that's alright as long as I can have one wish, I pray:**
> **When people look inside my life, I want to hear them say**
> **She's got her father's eyes. Her father's eyes.**
> **Eyes that find <u>the good in things</u>—when good is not around.**
> **Eyes that find the source of help, when help just can't be found.**
> **Eyes full of compassion, seeing every pain.**
> **Knowing what you're going through, and feeling it the same.**
> **Just like my father's eyes. Our Father's eyes. Just like our**
> **Father's eyes—**

Let us allow grace to set our hearts on fire; to reflect God's mercy— the Father's mercy. Here are some of the concrete examples of when we are the compassionate father:

- *Consoling:* a parent afflicted with Alzheimer's disease. Comforting the frustrated department store attendant, or the young couple separated by military duty.
- *Beseeching:* city planners to install traffic signals or to close a seedy bookstore. Curtailing the late-night revelers who waken our baby. We are called to be the Father.
- *Confronting:* building management to upgrade elder housing, the gang leader about neighborhood graffiti. Challenging our couch-potato relative to contribute their <u>talents</u> to the family.

We are called to be the Father.

- *Abiding*: with our child struggling with attention deficit. Disregarding the road-raged motorist who cuts us off, listening to the run-away teenager who rejects our values. We are the Father.

St. Augustine said: "Lord you made us for yourself. Our hearts are restless until they rest in you." The father's heart goes out to both sons. He desires to see them, different as they are, fed at the same table. In the same way, God chooses us. God calls us to become loving in the same way.

We manifest God's goodness by the way we treat others. In a world wracked by violence, we can make the mercy of God visible. And we validate God's promises in a world stripped of hope. The Holy Spirit will help us. Let us have the faith to do as the <u>prodigal</u> did. Let us "get up and go to the Father."

MY REFLECTION ____

____

____

FRIDAY

*Keep the main thing
the main thing.*

*What is the "main
thing" to me?*

Chapter Three
The Three Glances of Christ

The Three Glances of Christ Summary
Deacon Michael Thompson

What is a "Glance"? It is a quick look or snapshot in time where the eyes of one person looks through the eyes of another person and into their soul. A glance delivers a clear, concise message without using any words. In a marriage, often one spouse can communicate to the other spouse just by giving them a look. In the Gospel Scriptures, Jesus used glances several times to communicate a message to the heart of those to whom He was looking. In this Meditation, we examine three well-known times when Jesus used His glances to three different individuals.

The first "Glance" is to that of the rich, young man that asks Jesus, "Good teacher, what must I do to inherit eternal life?" Jesus tells him he must follow the commandments, to which the young man replies, "Teacher, all of these I have observed from my youth." Jesus then gives him the "Glance" of love and tells him that he is lacking only one thing. Jesus tells him to, "Go and sell what you have and give to the poor and you will have treasure in heaven." He then invites the young man to "then come, follow me." From that glance, the young man felt Jesus' love penetrating his soul. Despite this sincere feeling of love and this invitation from the Redeemer of the World, the young man is unable to let go of his possessions and do as Jesus said. From this story, the questions we ask ourselves are, " What are we unwilling to give up that is keeping us from becoming truly one with Jesus?" and, "Are we settling for a lesser good rather than having complete union with God?"

The second "Glance" is that of Jesus to Judas. Why Judas decided to betray Jesus we do not know, but Jesus knew all along that Judas would betray him. At any time, Jesus would have forgiven Judas. He even gave him one last chance when He said, "FRIEND, do what you have come for." By calling him friend, Jesus was trying to appeal to Judas to rethink what he was doing, and Jesus tried to give Judas a glance. It would have been a glance to make Judas pause and consider his actions. The problem was that Judas, being so involved in his sin, could not even look into the face of Jesus. He did not see the glance of Jesus that may have changed his course of action. Jesus had earlier told him, "But woe to that man by whom the Son of Man is betrayed. It would be better for that man if he had never been born." Even with, or maybe because of this warning, Judas misses the glance of Jesus. The question we should ask ourselves here is, " Are we despairing out of guilt instead of looking to Jesus for forgiveness, compassion, and healing?"

The third "Glance " is that of Jesus to Peter. Peter had sworn his allegiance to Jesus, stating he would be willing to die for Him. Jesus, knowing the human heart, warned Peter, "This very night before the cock crows twice you will deny me three times." When the soldiers came and arrested Jesus, Peter ran away, abandoning Jesus. Later, when Peter was warming himself by a fire in the courtyard, he was accused three times of being associated with Jesus. Peter denied it all three times. Just as he was making his third denial, the cock crowed. Immediately, Peter remembered what Jesus had said and looked toward Jesus; it was then that he received his glance from Jesus. Peter sees in the eyes of Jesus regret and sorrow, but also the mercy of God's forgiveness.

Unlike Judas, Peter was willing to look into the face of Jesus and accept the fact that he had let Jesus down. And, unlike Judas, Peter repented of this great offense and asked for mercy and forgiveness. Peter was forgiven and was later selected by God to lead the Church on Earth and become the first Pope after the resurrection of Jesus. It was the glance of Jesus that Peter received that led him not to despair, but to seek forgiveness and then do great work for God.

Christ is looking at each of us right now and looking on how we will respond. Will you look for the "Glance" of Jesus? Or will you be like the rich, young man, too afraid to let go of the things that are holding you back from loving Jesus completely? Or perhaps you will be like Judas, so caught up in your sin that you have your head down, avoiding the glance of Jesus as you dig deeper and deeper into sin? Or are you like Peter, sinful but repentant and seeking forgiveness, wanting a strong relationship with Jesus. You have a choice. Be like Peter!

MY REFLECTION ____________________________

____

____

Saviour and Jesus
Joan Tucker

I had gone ahead to the bathroom to get our son, Saviour's, water ready for his shower. Saviour was sitting with his Dad, Bill. If you have never read my book, *Saviour's Story*, let me fill you in briefly. Saviour was a "spirit child" Bill and I adopted from Ghana when I answered God's call to help Sister Stan in her orphanage, Nazareth Home for God's Children. He was born with cerebral palsy and still, after multiple operations, has trouble walking occasionally. Anyway, he was headed to the shower around 8 pm when he fell straight down for no apparent reason. Bill was immediately both hollering for me and trying to help Saviour. But Saviour had become rigid. When I got to him, I rolled him onto his side and started calling his name and touching his face. His eyes were open but they were going side to side or rolling upwards. I knew he needed immediate help. We called 911 and they responded quickly. He remained in this catatonic-like state for 50 minutes! He didn't respond until we were in the ER and they had drawn blood and had him hooked up to a variety of monitors.

It was then he shared with us the miracle he had just experienced. We were alone in the room with him, and he was now fully awake. Excitedly, he began to recount what had happened to him during that time he was unresponsive. He began by admitting that he could hear us when we were calling him, but he couldn't respond. You see, he was with Jesus and St. Michael!

Jesus was on one side of him and St. Michael on the other, and all 3 of three of them were walking. Saviour excitedly divulged he was clearly walking without his crutches! Saviour informed us that Jesus told him to always keep his eyes on Him. Saviour said that he, Jesus, and St. Michael spoke for a while, and then he was allowed to see things he had done in the past that he was instantly sorry for. He was teary-eyed as he spoke, telling us he made his confession to Jesus right then. I know when we confess to a priest we are confessing to Jesus, but confessing to Him face to face? My heart was pounding! Saviour couldn't describe much of the room they eventually were in, but he said it was full of angels. Then Jesus told Saviour that He was sending him back because he was needed, but Jesus wanted him to remember that He would always be right beside him wherever he went and to never be afraid!

Just last night at dinner, Saviour was still sharing details of his time with Jesus. I asked him if Jesus looked anything like Jonathan Roumie, who plays Jesus in The Chosen. Saviour laughed and replied, "No! Totally different! In heaven, their bodies have no hair, like on their chest and under their arms." This sparked a conversation between Bill and I about our "earth suits" and our heavenly bodies.

Bill and I still get teary-eyed as we think about Saviour's

experience. Our son was magnificently blessed with meeting Jesus face to face, made his confession to Jesus face-to-face, and was sent back to us to continue the mission for which he had been chosen – to live his life with his focus on Jesus. Our joy almost matches Saviour's! What a wonderful gift God had given us, again, in Saviour.

MY REFLECTION ____

____

____

My Fourth Day
Omar Rivera

I was born in Veracruz, Mexico and lived my Cursillo in 2008. The Cursillo of Christianity was a course that changed my life drastically, changed my way of thinking, my way of being, and most importantly, it changed my faith.

I was only 17 years old when I lived it. With the permission of both the parish priest and the spiritual guide, I was allowed to live my course at that age. My three days were an experience and an encounter with Christ from the first day. My heart was very broken and very hurt because I had recently gone through the separation of my parents. I spent a long time without talking to my mom for that reason, and I had a lot of resentment toward her. Although that was not the reason to go to the weekend, Cursillo helped me overcome and heal that stage of my life.

During the weekend, I was able to experience my first encounter with the Holy Spirit! I was able to know that it was an encounter with

Christ in the Blessed Sacrament and in the Eucharist. My first encounter with the Holy Spirit was during the holy hour. In my ignorance, I began to ask God for forgiveness for all my sins, then I recognized that without Him I was nothing. I gave up and asked him for strength, gave up all my problems, my worries and my thoughts! Suddenly I began to feel like something inside me ran through all my veins, my whole body, like a stream of water. I prayed for an hour without stopping. My body weakened and I became unconscious. I lost the notion of time, and when I woke up there was no one in the sanctuary of the church but God's presence, the spiritual Guide, and me. The Spiritual Guide asked me if everything was okay, and I told him that I had a lot of peace and that I did not know what had happened. He told me how happy I was because the Holy Spirit had manifested itself in me. I began to pray aloud and very quickly; I was sure nobody, if they heard, could understand anything. I began to tremble and fell asleep. I knew He was watching over me.

The first day I left the weekend, the Lord put it in my heart to go and reconcile with my mother, and I learned not to judge her. On Sunday, when I left the course, I arrived home at 11:00 pm. The first thing I did was go to see my mom and talk to her. It had been almost a year without me talking to her. I asked for forgiveness and told her that the Lord had changed my heart and that He had given me more love for her. We cried together, hugged and had a very long talk until about 2:00 am. It was a very beautiful experience I had with my mom. She told me that she didn't know what had happened to me, but that she wanted it to happen to her, too.

Now I can say my fourth day makes sense, because I know that I am not alone in this daily battle with Satan. Christ walks with me. I share my fourth day with my family, friends and acquaintances. My fourth day is simply to live in Christ and for Christ. In my Cursillo, I learned that in order to trust God I have to know who I am trusting and believing. My job has been to study the Bible, read books, and know my faith. As I grow in knowing and learning about my faith, I try to teach those around me. I like to learn about the Holy Scriptures and share them with others. I try to give them my verbal testimony, I try to give them my living testimony, to share my piety, (the love of Christ alive reflected in me), my study (the peace of the Lord through His Word) and my action (sharing the love and peace of the Lord). De Colores!

MY REFLECTION ____

____

____

The Three Glances Reflection
Sister Mary Epplin

Did you ever wonder what it was like for people in the Bible to actually <u>look at Jesus</u>? The gospels describe several times when Jesus <u>encountered someone</u>—face to face, eye to eye. I would like to reflect on <u>three</u> of those stories.

1. We call this first story: The <u>rich young man meets Jesus:</u> Mark 10:17-22

As Jesus was starting out on his way to Jerusalem, a man came running up to him, knelt down, and asked, "Good Teacher, what must I do to <u>inherit eternal life</u>?"

Jesus responded, "Why do you call me good? <u>Only God</u> is truly good. — But to answer your question: You know the commandments: 'You must not murder. You must not commit adultery. You must not steal. You must not testify falsely. You must not cheat anyone. Honor your father and mother."

"Teacher," the man replied, "I've obeyed all these commandments since I was young." Jesus looked at the man and felt <u>genuine love</u> for him. "There is still one thing more," Jesus told him. "Go and sell all your possessions. Give the money to the poor, and you will have treasure in heaven. Then come, <u>follow me</u>." At this, the man's face fell. He went away sad, for he had many possessions.

Now, here was a young man who was <u>very intelligent and hard-working</u>. He had <u>every</u>thing—prestige, privilege, and wealth. He managed his <u>finances</u> through hard work and clever investment, and he expected to obtain eternal life the same way—by doing all the <u>right things</u>. This young man was fascinated by Jesus' promise of eternal life. He felt drawn to this <u>unending bliss</u>. Imagine! Jesus was offering these treasures forever! So, he asks Jesus, "<u>What must I **do** to *gain* eternal life</u>?" Jesus reminds him, "Keep the commandments."

The young man thinks, *Well, <u>that</u> was easy!* And he confidently declares that he has <u>done that</u> all his life. Then, Jesus <u>looked</u> at him with love. Jesus must have seen the goodness in this man and sensed his great potential. But… Jesus also knew that the youth had to make <u>a change</u>.

"You <u>lack</u> one thing," Jesus challenged. "Go, sell what you own and give the money to the poor, and then <u>come, follow me</u>."

Give up everything? He just couldn't do it. Instead of taking a moment to reflect, the youth shrugged and slinked away. From that point, Jesus' loving gaze was <u>lost</u> on the young man—totally intent on securing what he <u>didn't</u> possess. Although Jesus had looked on him with love, the youth turned away. We can ask ourselves: "What do I have to leave behind to truly follow Christ?"

2. We call this <u>The woman at the well.</u> John 4:4-30

Jesus came to the Samaritan village of Sychar around noontime and sat wearily beside the well. His disciples had gone into the village to buy some food. Soon a Samaritan woman came to draw water, and Jesus said to her, "Please give me a <u>drink.</u>"

The woman was surprised because Jews have nothing to do with Samaritans. She said to Jesus, "You are a Jew, and I am a Samaritan woman. <u>Why</u> are you asking me for a drink?"

Jesus replied, "If you only knew the gift God has for you and who you are speaking to, you would <u>ask me</u>, and I would give you <u>living water</u>."

"Please, sir," the woman cried out, "Give me this water! Then I'll never be thirsty again, and I won't have to come here anymore to fetch water."

Jesus assured her, "…The Father seeks those who will worship him. God is Spirit, and those who worship him must worship in spirit and in truth."

The woman professed, "I know the Messiah is coming—the one who is called Christ. When he comes, he will explain everything to us."

Then Jesus told her, "<u>I</u> Am the Messiah!"

Many Samaritans from the village believed in Jesus because the woman had said, "He told me everything I ever did!"

Here Jesus, tired and sweating, encounters a woman drawing water at the hottest time of the day. Her lifestyle had earned her the brunt of neighborhood gossip. But Jesus gazes at her with love and understanding, and says, "If you knew the gift of God and who is speaking to you, you would ask him and <u>he would give you living water</u>."

Jesus patiently challenges her and gradually she draws near. She is moved from guilt and humiliation—to repentance. Jesus has offered her love and forgiveness. Running off to the village, she abandons her jar—and her sins— and announces that she has met the Messiah. By the loving glance of Jesus—that wonderful <u>encounter</u> with him—

she is transformed from a <u>sinful outcast</u> into a disciple <u>inflamed</u> with the desire to bring others to believe in Him.

For a moment, contrast the conversion of this Samaritan woman to others in the gospels: Judas, for example, one of the Lord's own apostles, <u>allowed greed, dishonesty and pride</u> into his soul, and fell into regret and despair over his guilt. And, Peter, who left everything to follow Jesus and even proclaimed Jesus as Messiah, but in <u>weakness betrayed him</u>. But in the end, the personal encounter and glance of Jesus, brought Peter to repentance.

3. We call this passage the <u>Woman who was crippled</u> Luke 13: 10-16

So, here's another story—again it's about a woman. But unlike the man, she was <u>not young</u>, and most likely <u>not rich</u>. Like the woman at the well, she too had <u>no status in the community.</u> Let's enter the scene.

We're in the synagogue on the Sabbath day where crowds of people are bustling about. There's a woman who was afflicted for many years with a crippling disease. She hides in the shadows to avoid attention.

Jesus looks up and sees her… His glance is full of compassion. He calls her to come closer. Picture the woman stumbling over to him, embarrassed before the crowd. Jesus reaches out and lays his hands on her. With a gentle face, <u>his eyes gaze at her</u>. "Woman, you are healed from your illness." With his touch, she <u>immediately</u> stood up straight and began <u>praising God</u>. For years she could see only the <u>ground</u> and people's dusty feet. But now, the first thing she sees is Jesus - his beautiful face, his sincere smile.

Imagine this woman scanning the people of the synagogue. After all those years, she could suddenly look at everyone eye to eye again. She could stand tall and take her place among the others with pride and confidence. Joyfully, she leaped and danced away!

We, too, look to Jesus for forgiveness, compassion, and healing. Yes, God is to be praised, and praised, and praised! The personal encounter and glance of Jesus!

There's a lot here to think about as we listen to Jesus' invitation. We can ask ourselves, "What does Jesus see <u>in me</u>? What response, what opportunities, is he calling me to?"

These three stories have one thing in common. Jesus invites three individuals, and each of us, to come nearer to him and to let go of anything that impedes that relationship. His loving glance tells us that he never asks the impossible but always gives the grace to respond in holiness and to become saints!

MY REFLECTION ______________________________________

____

____

Chapter Four
Ideal

Ideal Summary
Tommy Smith

Friday morning. First talk of the weekend. So, what is this going to be about and what is in it for me? Does this sound familiar to you? Was this your starting place? If it was, you joined other Cursillistas who thought the very same thing. If you recall, the talk started off with some very exciting things. You remember, I am sure, being excited to hear about rocks and trees and the animal kingdom. Since I would rather have my fingernails pulled out than to listen to a geology or biology lecture, I was wondering what in the world I had gotten myself into.

Then everything changed!

The crux of the first talk focused on the word "ideal." Ideal as in, "What motivates us? What gets us up in the morning? What centers us and gets us excited about life? What makes us passionate? What is the driving force of our being?" We learned, as you might recall, that our ideals in our life can and do change as we grow from a child to a young adult, to middle age, and beyond. We discovered we can have both false and authentic ideals. It also made sense that we can have ideals in every area of our lives: health, marriage, career, spirituality and more. And, although we may have these multiple ideals, we will eventually need to discover that one over-arching ideal that guides our entire life. (Hint: Jesus Christ) The talk moved us to imagine that an ideal was the direction in which we were trending, our North Star. We were reminded an ideal is necessary in our lives if our lives are to have purpose and meaning. Sometimes, we are very aware of our ideal and yet, many times, we are just blind to it. It was evident at this point that without an ideal, we would end up being driven by circumstance.

Now, with all this being said, the most important point of the talk came to us at the very end. So far, it had simply reminded us of the many lessons we had accumulated over our lives, about setting goals and directing our attention to our plans and the successful achievement of them. Not much new here but certainly a good reminder about priorities and why having direction in our life is important. But at this very juncture, the talk aimed an arrow right at our heart. We were asked, "What do you think about most of the time? What do you spend your money on? On what are your thoughts and energies mostly focused? What pleases and fulfills you most in life?" Our mind was now focused on the obvious answers to those questions and, just like you, we were told that in those answers, we would likely find our ideal. I knew the answers. I bet you did as well. Just like you, those answers provided clarity. We knew what our ideals were at that moment, and that gave us plenty to ponder. "Am I on the right path? What IS the meaning and direction of my life?" Those questions and their answers are still viable at this very moment, aren't they?

MY REFLECTION __________________________________

____

____

A Testimony That Attracts
Paula Belken

In 1986 I had a personal crisis. My marriage was falling apart, and I felt like a lost soul. My husband and I were unequally yoked; I was chasing Jesus and wanted a simple life, and he was chasing material goods beyond our financial capability to pay for them. I met Patrick and Robin, a couple at my church that had an extraordinary light in their faces and a serenity that seemed otherworldly. Their joy was so attractive that I craved their company like someone who was dying of thirst. They had a testimony that attracts. Most importantly, they noticed that I seemed lost and in need of a major dose of "Jesus."

They were music ministers, and when they found out that I like to sing, they invited me to sing with them at Mass and for any events where they were asked to provide music. Their friendship sustained me over the next two years as they prayed with me and invited me to spend time with them in adoration before the Blessed Sacrament. I was often so distraught I couldn't even find the words to pray. They would kneel with me between them before the Blessed Sacrament and pray the words that were locked up in my heart. Matthew 18:20 "For where two or three are gathered in my name, there I am in the midst of them."

At their urging I asked my husband to participate in marriage and financial counseling, which he refused. Finally, under the crushing weight of debt with no promise to change the behavior that created it, I packed up and went home to my parents. I filed for divorce.

In 1988, Patrick and Robin invited me to attend a Cursillo weekend. It was there that I became infused with the same light and joy of Christ that I had seen in their faces. In 1989, when the divorce was final, I began the annulment process. I was 31, a single mother with a deep desire to find a Godly man to be the spiritual head of our family. I lamented this to Patrick, who replied, "Right now, you just need to focus on Paula and Jesus."

1 Corinthians 1:9 says: "God is faithful, and by him you were called to fellowship with his son, Jesus Christ our Lord." I prayed very specifically for the kind of man I desired for a husband. He needed to be kind, gentle, thoughtful, patient, even-tempered, a good steward, generous, and a practicing Catholic. I figured I was asking for a miracle.

I prayed the rosary every night, seeking Mary's intercession. If Jesus' mother could convince him to turn water into wine, she could ask him to find me a husband with these qualities.

The mercy of the Lord knows no limit. God provided a man with every specification, with patience being especially important, as I needed the annulment before we could be married in the church! We were married in October of 1991. Thanks to the Holy Family, I have a husband who is a Cursillista seeking to walk the path of holiness with me, five beautiful grown children and five grandchildren.

"Ask, and it shall be given you; seek, and ye shall find; knock, and it shall be opened unto you:" ~ Matthew 7:7

MY REFLECTION ____

____

____

Crossroads
Marianne Joy

I lived my Cursillo weekend in 2012 in the Diocese of Metuchen, NJ. I served on team for the first time the following year and I was given the first rollo, *Ideal*. When I was first given this assignment, I remember thinking, people don't really talk about the concept of Ideals; it's not something we hear in everyday conversation. Coincidentally, I then stumbled upon a quote which really got my attention:

"You need an ideal, something that will draw you out of yourself and raise you to greater heights."

Nine years later, I moved from Hillsborough, New Jersey to Conway, South Carolina. My first time on team here, I was once again assigned the Ideal rollo. A lot had happened in my life in those nine years. I knew I wanted to share this beautiful quote again, but I wasn't sure where I was going with the rest of the rollo.

Around that time, I took a trip back to Hillsborough and, the morning I left to come home, I started thinking about my being at a crossroads… And there I was at that moment in time caught between two worlds… my old life in New Jersey, which was comfortable, safe and familiar, and the new one, here in South Carolina.

As I drove the ten hours to come home, I started thinking, what is my ideal at this point in my life? And, suddenly, as I was driving, the Holy Spirit filled my head and heart, and my rollo fell into place:

My personal experience is that sometimes life throws you curve balls and takes you places where you don't necessarily want to go. So you just have to move forward... I am 64 years old and I realized that there is so much more for me to do. And that I'm never too old to continue this journey.

In the past, I was like a sailor without a compass. I realize that I may not have all the answers now, but I finally had both hands on the rudder. I've also learned to make the most of the journey. I appreciate the sun and the wind on my face as I set sail on the sea toward the horizon; I learned that persevering through unexpected storms makes me stronger and, occasionally, I get to see a rainbow... As I sail on this sea of life, I'm steering the mainmast of my little sailboat toward the destination that defines who I am today... and where I want to be... tomorrow. And I asked myself, what can I do to make this world we live in "an ideal world"?

You may wonder who the author of the Ideal quote is. When I first read the quote in 2013, I learned that it was written by Blessed

Elizabeth of the Trinity. I had never heard of her before, and I read everything I could about her. As the Cursillo weekend drew near, I remember wondering what her Feast day was. I looked it up and learned that it is November 9. When I looked at the calendar, I discovered that I would be presenting my first-ever rollo… on Elizabeth's Feast day!

Elizabeth was canonized in 2016. Here is the rest of the quote, which fascinated me so much that I needed to know more about her. She quickly became one of my favorite saints.

"You need an ideal, something that will draw you out of yourself and raise you to greater heights. But you see, there is only one; it is he, the Only Truth! …he fascinates, he sweeps you away; under his gaze the horizon becomes so beautiful, so vast, so luminous."

MY REFLECTION _______________________________________

____

____

Living My Ideal
Liliana Tinoco Osorio

I am 38 years old and originally from Córdoba Veracruz, Mexico. I am currently single with four beautiful children. Two women and two men who are the most beautiful gift that GOD MY HEAVENLY FATHER has lent me. I lived my Cursillo from March 28 to 31, 2018 in North Carolina, number 143 and I am named Our Lady of Fatima.

When I heard about the Cursillo, I was very curious. The priest invited us after Mass and I asked, what is it about and he answered, "I invite you to the Ultreya next Friday and there you can get an idea of what is the Cursillo." As they say, curiosity kills the cat and I went. What I never imagined was that, after going to that Ultreya, a new life for me would begin.

Many things were happening. I was pregnant and my baby was born on September 11, 2018. The day of the course was approaching and my baby was just four months old. I hesitated attending because he was very small. My mom convinced me to go and said she would take care of him. The first night I was there, it was something beautiful. I had gone to other retreats but what I was starting to live was simply fascinating, at least that's how I was feeling. As the days passed, I continued being fascinated by everything I was learning. I thought that I knew GOD, but it was not true. I realized that not only did He give up his only Son to save us from our sins, but that it was the beginning of a new life. Every word I heard from Sister Martha was as if she knew everything about me and she was speaking directly to me. What struck me the most was when she told me that I was a daughter of God who loved me, and I had to value myself, and respect myself, because He had given his life *for me!* That stayed in my mind and in my heart, and there began my (METANOIA) change of mind and heart. During those three days, I learned more about God than in my whole life, and from there began my fourth day.

After those three beautiful days I lived, I thought everything was going to be different. I quickly realized that everything was the same and that I had a lot of work to do, mainly at home and in my workplace, my square meter. I began to serve more in my parish by being a minister of the Word, and I am currently working on the Postcursillo (my fourth day) by increasing and promoting the Christian conversion through Cursillo. I was put in charge of new Cursillistas and motivating them to continue living the Grace of God by attending friendship groups, Ultreyas, and School of Leaders.

Everything was going very well until the pandemic arrived.

Churches closed and we could not meet as usual, but we were in mutual agreement that we would meet by zoom or What's App and so we continued. Unfortunately, everything got worse; first, I lost my dear mother-in-law. I also lost two very important people in my life, my uncle whom I loved so much and my mother in a week's time. It seemed as if I was living a nightmare, but my friendship group was always there with me giving me encouragement. I never thought something like this would happen to me, and I questioned God about everything that was happening.

I dealt with a terrible depression, and I did not know how to get out of it. Carmen, Delmys, Delia, Argelia, and Janeth were always there pushing me, and if it had not been for God's mercy and the support of all of them, who knows where I would be now?

I remember the day I went to say goodbye to them. I was leaving. I no longer wanted to belong to Cursillo. I felt I was taking for granted everything that I learned in those three days and I didn't want to continue. I was mad with the world, with the Church and with God. I felt that the only way to get out of my depression, was to get away from everything. I was jealous when others laughed and seemed happy, I was drowning in my sadness, especially when the team members told me to be strong and that God was with me. I wondered why wasn't He with my Mom? Why didn't He heal her when she was dying? As they were leaving the friendship meeting, Carmen called me over and asked if I wanted to serve on the women's Cursillo team for the Diocese of Raleigh, NC. I answered that I would think about it. I no longer wanted to know anything about the Church, nothing about the course and, while driving back home, I asked God, "Why me?" I said to HIM, "If I blamed you for the death of my mother, if I doubted your love, I feel bad. Forgive me." I arrived at my house, and I started to read my Cursillo notes and found some questions that were asked of us. They were:

1. What is your ideal?
2. What is your dream for your life?

3.   How do you imagine yourself in 5 years?

Then, I remembered my answers, but the most important one was the answer to the last question. I said that I would be serving in some capacity and that someday God would give me the privilege of serving on a Cursillo weekend, and that's what I had asked for. Then I understood that everything has a why, and a purpose. All the teachings of my mother to love God and to obey Him came full circle. But, above all, to accept His will. I accepted the opportunity to serve on the team and gave my first rollo.

I was able to serve with five wonderful women who are now part of my life and help me grow more as a woman. They saw in me a friend who was fighting every day to do better after losing my Mom and giving it my best. I realized that God has a purpose for me and it is to serve no matter how or to whom, as long as it is with much love. I always remember a phrase of Saint Mother Teresa of Calcutta, "He who does not live to serve, does not serve to live," and it is very true. Now, I only ask God to give me strength to follow His call. While it is not easy, neither is it impossible when we put God first.

I fight daily to be a better mother, better sister, and better human being, and to be an example for others in the way I live my own life. Understand that you can be better with that conviction as well. Each day we have the opportunity to realize our own possibilities and become a better person by helping others to do the same because ... Christ and I are an overwhelming Majority. De Colores!

MY REFLECTION ____

____

____

Chapter Five
Habitual Grace

Habitual Grace Summary
Deacon Coleman Parks

We all search for something more than what this world offers because that's exactly how God made us – how He wired us. That "something more" that everyone is looking for is simply *finding God*. Our Bible, our history books, and last night's news make it clear that the world is a distracting and tempting place. While filled with many wonderful things, it is also a world full of danger and trouble, things that can cause us to lose our way back to God. The sad truth is that many people in this world today are so preoccupied with this physical world, they have either lost interest in finding God or have little or no time for God. Because of that state of mind, they miss the greatest gift God wants to give us, and that undeserved gift is God's Grace. It is a permanent gift, totally free and unmerited, given out of love for us.

The first effect of this Grace is sanctification; thus, Sanctifying Grace and Habitual Grace are one and the same in that they make us partakers of God's nature. Simply because of His great love for us, God gives us this undeserved GIFT of Himself, and it is this Grace that enables us to respond to His call to become His children and pleasing to Him. Through this gift of Grace, we share in the divine nature of God Himself. All we must do is accept it! When we are baptized, God infuses His Grace, His very life in us, and He will always be there, even when we might choose to disregard Him. But God desires that His place in the soul grows and flourishes until it envelops and permeates everything in the life of the Christian until living in the right relationship with Him becomes a habit. Thus, Habitual Grace.

The soul is cleansed of sin through Grace, and therefore sin and Grace cannot coexist in the soul. It is through Grace that we become pleasing to God. It is Grace that helps us realize the plans of mankind will never be as good as the plans of God. But in creating all of us, God gave us a challenge by blessing and cursing us with a free will spirit. Every day we must make choices, choices between things of this world or things of God. The Good news of the Holy Gospel is that God so loves all of us that He is constantly trying to help us, constantly reaching out to us with His love and that love is His Grace.

God wants to give us Grace upon Grace yet, we still must open our hands and hearts to receive it. There is an abundance of Grace available to us through the Word of God, the Sacraments, particularly the Eucharist, and prayer - all of which can help lead us to personal conversion IF we are willing to make them daily practices in our lives. We must strive for personal maturity in faith, greater trust in God, and a disciplined conviction to sin no more.

I personally strive every day to move from living a life of sporadic Grace to one of Habitual Grace. I constantly strive to create more and more activities that bring Grace to my daily life. These activities need to be routine, and that's not easy to do because the devil is constantly at work, tempting and distracting us. But we all can do it if we simply replace self-centered, destructive habits with God-centered ones. All things are possible with God.

My wife Barbara, one of God's blessings upon me, was far ahead of me in her dedication to God. She has always inspired me to pray and to be a better Catholic. From working the church picnics to joining the Knights of Columbus to becoming a lector, doing God's work led me to discernment in 1996, and in 2002, I was ordained a Deacon in the Catholic Church. It remains my greatest accomplishment in life due solely to the Grace of God, a God who never gave up on me. I was simply another one of God's miracles, albeit a big one.

My loving father died a year after I married my wife Barbara. Sixteen years later I was ordained. On the Sunday morning when I celebrated my first Mass, my dear Irish mother told me, "You know, you should go out to the cemetery today and visit your father's grave. You'll recognize the spot because the grass is all curled up where your father rolled over in his grave when he found out you became a Deacon!" How great and forgiving is our God, and how powerful and amazing is His Grace!

Lastly, when Habitual Grace becomes a permanent disposition to live and act in relationship with God, we discover that our individual life is more and more conformed to God's Will. It is not as though we give up our own will; it is just that we find joy in the realization that we are living out the prayer, "Thy will be done on earth as it is in heaven." As St. Paul writes to the Galatians, "I have been crucified with Christ; yet I live, no longer I, but Christ lives in me." This is the joy and exultation of the saints. This is the goal of holiness – a perfect union with the Will of God, just like Jesus.

Living in Habitual Grace has enabled me to have greater trust in God's plans, even when they don't seem like they are working. I've had near-death car wrecks, bodily injuries, a son who was an alcoholic, and another son with a heroin addiction. But through it all, I have never had a crisis of faith because God always gave me enough Grace to not only survive but to prosper. Today. because of God's Grace, I have those two sons, alive and well and prospering, all because of God's Grace.

God has a plan for all of us, a plan that is bigger than we can ever comprehend, and I am certain His plan will always be better than ours. Grace is not given to "change us." It is given to remind us that we have been created in the image and likeness of God; we are His adopted children; we are brothers and sisters of Christ. As such, we are heirs to Heaven. What greater gift can there be?

____

____

Goat Ministry
Bill Thomas

In my past life, I was a middle school math teacher. My subject was math but my job was to teach kids. I loved my students and I worked hard to teach them to think. I not only wanted them to think and do well in math, but I also wanted them to use their reasoning ability to make good choices — in what they said, in what they did, and in how they treated others. I always tried to set a good example, and if I messed up I tried to apologize and to explain what I should have done or said. I wanted my kids to always apply logic and reasoning, compassion and respect to whatever they did.

Then, I retired and no longer had students. My daughter thought I needed something else to do, so she gave me two Nigerian Dwarf doelings — goat kids to replace my school kids.

Those two little goats grew up and had babies and their babies had babies and in a few years and several generations later I had over two dozen goats, but I didn't get to see very many people. Along came Covid and I was even more isolated. I saw masked workers at the feed store and my wife and that was about it. I felt as the evangelization leg of my tripod had been amputated.

I began milking my goats and I put up a sign on the road advertising raw milk and cheese. It started slowly but a few brave people began to drive in. I began selling some milk, selling some cheese, but best of all, I got to talk to people. I enjoyed showing off my herd and answering questions. I explained the health benefits of goat milk and offered samples of milk and cheese. I most liked it when people brought their children. I was always respectful, friendly, and kind, and I tried to give them something to think about.

I got some regular customers and they gradually became friends. One lady, Sara, would come every week and she always wanted to play with the goats. She began bringing her adult daughter. Each week they would come and spend thirty minutes to an hour with my "kids." Sometimes they just came for the visit and didn't even get any milk. On one visit Sara's daughter took me aside and told me that her mom was very different at home. Her husband had recently died and she was pretty depressed. When she was with the goats was the only time that she was happy and acted like her old self. My wife began calling my goats a "ministry".

Another customer, Don, a pretty frail-looking guy, said he wanted to start drinking goat's milk for health reasons. He explained that he had been sick and had lost about fifty pounds. The doctors weren't sure what was wrong or what to do about it. He was also losing vision in one eye and was really weak. He had read about goat's milk and wanted to try it. He started with one quart but was soon up to three quarts a week. He would call me when he was coming and I would wrap his milk and take it to him in his truck. He was so rundown that it was hard for him to get up the porch steps and three quarts was a load to carry. As he told me about his problems, I said I hoped the milk would help and that I would pray for him. Each week he would tell me of any new problems or small improvements, and I would always tell him I was still praying.

One day, when I said I was praying, Don said, "Bill, you know I don't believe in God." He told me about his childhood and why he figured that God did not exist. I listened and when he finished I told him I would still pray. I felt that the third leg of my tripod had begun to grow again.

Three years later, Don has gained back about forty pounds, has seen marked improvement in his vision and has gotten his energy back. He is making plans for what he will do in retirement. He has some property in North Carolina and plans to get some chickens and goats and… he laughed, "become another Bill."

In addition to the seventy-some people who have purchased milk and cheese, my milk has helped feed several litters of pups and kittens, a couple of orphaned deer fawns, has been made into soap and lotion, and has been fed to babies in place of formula. My favorite story along those lines is of a two-month-old baby who could not keep breast milk down and was not gaining weight. Dad said the doctor wanted to put him on special formula but he wanted to try goat's milk first. He bought a quart and came back a week later. He said they had gradually shifted to the goat's milk and his son has quit spitting up. He asked me to freeze three gallons to go with his wife when she went back to Alabama to close on the sale of their previous home. About a month later, he came back for another three gallons. He said his boy has gained five pounds.

All these people, their kids, and their pets have enjoyed the produce from my goats, and I have enjoyed many hours of conversation. I've bragged on my kids, answered lots of questions, told a few jokes, and made many new friends. Even though the sales of milk and cheese sometimes don't cover the cost of the feed, and my goat account is often in the red, my tripod is back in better balance.

I guess, if you are open to it, you can bloom where you are planted, even if it is in a lonely goat pasture.

MY REFLECTION ____

____

____

And Now, The Rest of the Story (Thanks, Mr Harvey)
Bill Thomas

After I had written and submitted "Goat Ministry," Don's story had another chapter.

One Saturday, Don didn't come for his usual five quarts of milk. Sunday, Monday, and I didn't hear from him. Tuesday and Wednesday and still no word. I decided to call to see if he was alright. I didn't want to sound like I was pressuring a customer, but... Don's secretary answered his personal phone and said he was in the hospital for a procedure but would not tell me anymore. Of course, I upped the "Don Prayers" that day.

Several more days went by and I called again but got no answer. I called several more times over the following couple of weeks — I even tried his business phone — but no one ever answered. Finally, I quit calling. Maybe he had decided to move to North Carolina sooner than he had planned. I didn't know where Don was, even if he was still alive. As he was a self-professed non-believer, I prayed that he would be, or had been, given a chance to reconsider. "God, give Don a second chance."

Time passed and six weeks after Don had disappeared, he called me! "Hi, Bill. I just got out of the hospital. If you have any milk I'll come get it tomorrow. I'll talk to you then." They arrived as promised. Don's wife was chauffeuring; Don just sat in the truck. He was back down to one hundred forty pounds and was very weak. He spoke clearly but had trouble finding some of the words he wanted to say. He told me that the Saturday after he had come for milk the last time, he had begun feeling bad. He drove himself to Urgent Care but could not even get out of his truck. Someone noticed him and helped him inside and that was the last that he remembered for weeks. (Later Don's son told me that the doctors thought that Don would probably not live for more than a couple weeks.) But he did! He retired, and his wife took over running the business. He resumed drinking his five quarts of goat milk each week.

After a few weeks, Don was given the okay to drive again, and he was gaining strength and weight. One day he was strong enough to climb the steps to our porch, and we had a chance to sit and talk. After a few minutes of just random friendly conversation, Don got a little more intense and he asked me, "Bill, do you know of any churches around here that are preaching the Bible?"

The question took me off guard. I didn't understand what he meant. He explained that he had been listening to a podcast by a preacher who was discussing the prophecies and predictions of the Bible. The Reverend was working through Revelations and relating it to current events and to the "end times." Don said he wanted my opinion. He said, "You know a lot about the Bible and you help me understand it — you explain it in plain language" (made me feel good and inadequate at the same time).

I listened to several podcasts over the next couple of weeks, and Don and I talked about them. We had some great discussions. Also, Don said he had talked to his adult sons about this. One said he wasn't interested and the other one said, "Welcome aboard, Dad." Don was trying to reconcile with his brothers and sister, too. They had had a problem in a joint business relationship and had not spoken for several years. Further, Don said he was cleaning up his language.

Don and I continued our discussions. We talked about forgiveness of sin. Don couldn't understand why Catholics confess to a priest instead of going directly to Jesus. We also talked about saints, and the "Real Presence." He had lots of questions.

My "Don prayers" were changing again. Of course, I prayed that he would continue to regain his health and that he'd continue to grow in his faith, but also that I could keep up with him and help him "think through" his faith and his relationship with God. Don is a thinker.

The last time we talked I detected some concerns on Don's part that maybe I wasn't as "saved" as he had thought. He kept emphasizing that Jesus was the source of mercy and forgiveness and we really didn't require a priest to forgive us. Also, he wanted to make sure I trusted in the "real" Bible. "You know, Bill, the Catholic Bible has some differences from my real one."

I asked Don a couple of questions. First, about confessing to a priest. Why did Jesus tell the apostles, "Whatever sins you declare bound on earth shall be bound in heaven and whatever sins you declare loose on earth shall be loosed in heaven." Secondly, the Catholic Bible is the one that was written by the apostles. Why would changes, made hundreds of years after it was written, make the Bible more authentic and better? These were new thoughts to Don. As he left, he said he was going to research these points. As Don keeps learning and growing in his faith, I believe the Holy Spirit is rewarding his honest quest for truth and his search for a relationship with Christ. Don keeps thinking.

I wonder if someday I will get to sponsor him on his Cursillo weekend. Anyway, in Don's case, I added a step to our Cursillo mantra. "Make a friend, sell him goat milk, be a friend, and…"

MY REFLECTION ____

____

____

No Need to Fear
Alejandra Garcia Hernandez

I lived my Cursillo February 10-13, 2022. My experience was lovely. I learned many things I didn't know, especially knowing that the only one who doesn't judge you is God.

My 4th day has provided me with many blessings, not necessarily easy because we will always be battling the enemy who wants us to fail. However, having God in your heart and holding his hand will allow you to see and feel the beauty of His love. His love also allows us not to fall and to make it easier to make better decisions.

Everything I have learned has shown me that God will always be by your side. And one thing you should remember is that you will always be loved and protected by Him. No need to fear. De Colores!

MY REFLECTION ____

____

____

Purpose Driven Life
Marianne Joy

Some of you may be thinking, "I'm not comfortable talking to people, especially about my faith." When I sat where you're sitting now, ten years ago, I thought the same thing. My whole life I was a ridiculously shy person, uncomfortable in crowds, tongue-tied around strangers, and I would NEVER get up and speak in front of a crowd like this. But I was transformed on that three-day weekend in 2012, and my life has never been the same since.

I remember reading a book called A Purpose Driven Life by Rick Warren, and I thought to myself, "I want to do these things." But I didn't know how to go about it. Although I attended Mass weekly, and I read my Bible daily, I was not strong in my faith. I had so much to learn.

But I had received so much grace on that weekend. I was transformed, but I knew I had a lot more to do to amend my life.

Shortly after my Cursillo weekend, God began to work in my life in many visible ways. I was determined to live my life proclaiming God's glory, and telling others about His love for them and how He transformed my life. And I think when you're passionate about a subject, you just want to tell the whole world! I began to live a purpose-driven life with great joy.

This joy must have been quite evident. I used to have ongoing conversations with a former coworker. Cathy (not her real name) has really had it tough the past few years. I don't know of too many people whose lives are challenged by an overabundance of suffering, seemingly endless long-suffering, but she's one of them. She has fibromyalgia and is in severe chronic pain. She went through a nasty divorce and lost her home along with everything she had.

Many afternoons during work, I would take a break and go to the Blessed Sacrament Shrine a few blocks away from where I worked. I would bring back prayer cards for Cathy. They always put a smile on her face. I encouraged her to go back to church and to confession. I gave her the link to the church near her home with the schedule for confession as well as instructions just in case she was rusty.

Over the years, I gave Cathy invitations to various events. She never came, but I never gave up. One day I sent her the link to a Zoom event for my church's Women's Group. Dr. Edward Sri, one of my favorite Catholic speakers and authors, was our guest speaker. To my surprise, I saw Cathy there! But then she was gone. I figured she was tired after working all day. Then I got a text that she could see everybody but she couldn't hear. So, I asked her, "Would you like me to call you and you can listen in?" She said yes! She stayed on until the very end. Afterward, she texted to thank me. She said she had already downloaded one of his books on Kindle.

"You must be exhausted," I told her.

"I am, but my mind is going," she said, "so I'm making a cup of tea, and I'm going to think about what I heard." And she thanked me again.

And then I moved here to South Carolina. I tried to stay in touch and we would text back and forth, but then I would call her and it always went to voicemail and she wouldn't call me back. In January, she texted me and asked, "Can you help me? What kind of Bible do I get?"

Well, I picked up the phone and this time she answered! We had a wonderful, long conversation. I told her of a few Bibles that I know of but I said, it doesn't matter, just make sure that it's Catholic, or you will be missing some of the books. I suggested a reading plan for her. I asked her if she had been going to church. She said no, she didn't feel comfortable around people. So, I told her that the church near her house has 24/7 Adoration. I told her it's usually not crowded, and she will be in the presence of Jesus in the Blessed Sacrament. I'm praying that Cathy will make it back to church. We may be miles apart, but she knows I'm always here for her.

There are so many other examples where I have been able to witness in the workplace. I know it's not easy, and we must be cautious in a secular environment, but if the people around you see that you live your faith, God will provide opportunities for conversation. Remember, Jesus didn't hang around just with the pious; He placed Himself smack in the center of people who didn't know much about God and who needed to learn about His love and mercy. And I'm living proof.

MY REFLECTION ____

____

____

Into the Pool, Anyone?
Sister Mary Frances Epplin

Our grace-filled relationship with God is <u>somewhat like swimming!</u> Swimming, our health care team reminds me often, provides cardio-vascular health, and builds balance, flexibility, and endurance. But, once you arrive at the pool with its refreshing water, high dive, and jacuzzi, there's a choice. You can stand on the sidelines, clutching an inner tube, and … **watch…** <u>Or</u> you can **<u>jump in,</u>** paddle, float, splash, and enjoy the exercise!

God's grace, a gift of the Holy Spirit, gives us <u>discernment</u> in our relationship with God and prepares us to live and act in keeping with God's call. ***Habitual grace,*** also called sanctifying grace, is <u>God's love</u> pouring into our lives. <u>Habitual grace</u> continues our baptismal work of holiness, leads us to the intimate life of the blessed Trinity, and heals our wounds of original sin—so that we can live in union with God.

So, God's grace is <u>not like a commodity,</u> limited by supply and demand. God's grace is <u>not "rewards points"</u>—where you have to save them until you really need them, or for a special occasion.

God's grace is <u>not</u> like a baseball game: three strikes and you're out.

God's grace is more like <u>unlimited minutes in a mobile phone plan.</u> You might say that—at baptism, we begin the "anytime, anywhere, unlimited minutes plan."

And it's free!

Grace is from the Greek word *charis,* which means <u>gift,</u> charism, or friendship with God. By nature, grace

is <u>permanent</u>—but the <u>bond</u> of grace may be broken//
temporarily, or forever, if we abuse our free will through sin.

But when we cherish and guard grace in our soul, we have a
<u>trust-worthy pledge of everlasting life</u> with God.

Have you ever heard the story of ***Servant of God, Elisabeth
Leseur?*** Young Elisabeth married Dr. Felix Leseur, but discovered that
he was a non-believer who detested the Church. Despite his promises
to respect her faith, Felix filled his library with atheistic literature.
Elisabeth, however, collected Catholic classics and the lives of the saints.

In 1912, even as Elizabeth was dying at the age of 46, Felix
persisted, "I've sworn hatred of God, I shall live in that hatred and I
shall die in it." Still, Elizabeth offered her sufferings for his conversion.

Later, Dr. Leseur visited Lourdes, <u>intending to discredit the
miraculous shrine</u>. Instead, he felt the conviction of Elizabeth's sacrifices
and contemplation of Christ's sufferings. Dr. Leseur's resistance to God
<u>crumbled</u>—and in 1923, at the age of 62, he was ordained a Catholic priest.

Elisabeth's love responded to sanctifying grace— God's habitual
grace—and brought redemption for her husband.

***Our Supreme Ideal is Life in Grace. No matter where I am or what I
do, Christ will always offer his unfailing gift of grace.***

MY REFLECTION ______________________________________

____

____

Chapter Six

Layperson in the Church/World

Layperson in the World/Church Summary
Sharon Shymansky Roberts

I remember waking up the Friday morning of my Cursillo weekend well-rested. I had been given an actual roll-away bed, as I had recently had knee surgery, and it was the first bed as you entered the sleeping area, so I felt isolated from most of the group. If I slept on my right side, no one was in my line of vision. I was the closest person to the chapel, which I took as a good sign that my wish of meeting Jesus face-to-face this weekend would be fulfilled. Maybe today would be the day!

Morning prayer, meditation, and talks filled the morning. We had lunch and then reconvened. It was then this rollo was given. It was then I learned the consecration of the world depended on me. (Thankfully, not just me, but me and the rest of my Catholic brothers and sisters – the Laity). (Pope Pius the XII – *The consecration of the world depends on the layperson*). It was then I learned that God was asking me to be His hands and feet and voice. "Oh boy!" I remember thinking, "God's mission of bringing the world to Christ is in trouble if it's in *my* hands!"

The speaker then recounted all the problems the world is facing. While listening, I was tempted to spiral into desolation, but the speaker quickly identified the cause *and* the solution. The root of the world's problems lies in its separation from God; our world has turned its back on our Creator. The solution, then, is simple – Jesus Christ and His Church.

You learned, as I did that day, that the Church is much more than a building. It is the people inside who are the Church and who make her come alive. I am the Church, you are the Church, WE are the Church! We learned that inside that Church, two separate entities exist, and while both are on the same team, God's team, their missions are different.

First, there is the Clergy, whose mission is to transform people through God's Grace. Second, is the Laity, whose mission is to transform the world by living in that Grace, to go beyond the walls of the Church and live among family, friends, co-workers, and strangers. The world is searching for happiness, and as Christians, it is our responsibility to bring it to them and lay it at their feet. The happiness they seek, however, only Christ can give. As Laity, we are called to share it with everyone, but each person must accept the gift of Christ on his own.

The speaker spoke about what the layperson is NOT to clearly define LAITY. The layperson is neither Clerical nor Anti-Clerical. Clerical refers to those laypersons who appear to worship the priest, often to the point of giving more credence to what the priest says than to the Word of God. Those in this category are often all talk and no action. On the opposite spectrum are the Anti-Clerical, those laypeople who do not like and respect the clergy simply because they ARE clergy.

"Then, what is the layperson?" you may have asked. Ahh. The Laity are those people in Church who imagine and live their lives in the world according to Christ. They are tasked to not only spread the Good News of the Gospel but truly live that message. It's more than just speaking about Christ. It's being so enmeshed in Him and your love of Him that He flows out of you wherever you go. He is in your eyes, the radiance of your face, the excitement in your words. His joy pours out of you onto all whom you meet.

What does this mission of the Laity look like? We learned there are four telling attributes. Can you find yourself in each of them?

1- Human - Are you putting your gifts and talents at the service of Christ to spread His kingdom?

2- Supernatural – Are you living life to the fullest and being the best version of yourself, as Matthew Kelly puts it?

3- Ecclesial – Are you working with the clergy to build His

kingdom? Both the clergy's mission and ours must work in perfect synchrony to build it!

4- Apostolic – Are you His apostolate, concerned about the salvation of those around you?

How did you do when you heard all this? Did you resolve right then to actively be the hands, feet, and face of Christ as the Cursillo Cross asks us to be? John XXIII stated: The Christian is a joy, a joy to himself, to God and to his fellow men."

Oh, about meeting Jesus face-to face that weekend? Turns out something much better occurred, though not until early Sunday morning, when I awoke filled with incredible and unexplainable joy! I ran, pajama-clad, into the chapel and there, with the first hints of early morning light caressing the altar's crucifix, I met Jesus **heart-to-heart**. (So much better than face-to-face!) I was filled with His love, but more than that, I was overflowing with a love *for* Him, a love I had often questioned. Did I love Him enough? Was I enough for Him? That Sunday morning, the answer to both questions was a resounding and deafening YES. I am a beloved daughter of THE KING!

MY REFLECTION ____

____

____

Praying for Others
Debra Layer

Some Cursillista friends shared with me a recent experience of theirs. Their efforts at spontaneous evangelization were effective, and I wanted to see if my prayer partners and I could successfully experience this as well, as we are all called to be Christ to others whenever and wherever we can.

I joined five of my prayer partners at a local barbecue restaurant for lunch. I told them ahead of time that I wanted our group to pray for our server at the end of the lunch, if our server was agreeable. My prayer partners wholeheartedly agreed to join me and support my effort.

The restaurant was crowded, and our server was very busy. She stopped by our table one final time and asked if there was anything else she could do for us. I casually said, "Why yes, there is." I asked our server if there was anything on her heart that she would like our prayer group to pray for. She looked shocked at our request and immediately teared up. She shook her head yes emphatically, mentioning that her son had recently left the family home in anger, and she was very worried about him.

Our server left our table, and we immediately prayed for her and her son individually, as well as a group. Each of us, both individually and as a group, considers this encounter as an overwhelmingly positive experience. It took little time and cost us nothing, but it apparently made a huge impact on our server as well as on each of us.

MY REFLECTION ____

____

____

Serve with Humility
Andrea Marcella

One of my talents is cooking. I love to cook and bake. On Cursillo weekends, I have been the kitchen coordinator many times.

It is very hard work, but I always enjoy it. My problem is, I don't take compliments well. When someone compliments me on food I have prepared, I become embarrassed. I'm trying very hard to overcome this by remembering that God gave me this talent, and I need to use it for His glory.

What a blessing it is to make people happy by feeding them! Humility doesn't mean putting ourselves down in public. Humility is recognizing that each person, regardless of what they may appear to be, has a special talent that is exclusively theirs. I'm reminded of a poster that reads: "God don't make no junk."

Humility nourishes all the other virtues. The proud person sees herself as a source of her talents with the right to use them as she sees fit. The humble person recognizes God as the source and accepts the responsibility to use God's gifts well. I was given a plaque that reads: "I asked God for all things that I may enjoy life. He gave me life that I may enjoy all things."

So, search for and celebrate the gifts God has given YOU, and then use them humbly to serve His people and glorify Him. That is what we are called to do.

MY REFLECTION ____

____

____

The Story of Anna
Sharon Thomas

Anna was on the dark side of life. She was a drug addict,

homeless, married and divorced three times, rejected by her family, and without any good friends. When she was homeless in Idaho, she had lived in a car in the parking lot of a Catholic Church. Since the people were so nice to her, were not judgmental, and let her use the bathroom by the Adoration Chapel, she decided to look into becoming a Catholic. Anna had been raised Baptist and baptized with full immersion. This was a leap of faith, for sure, but she was unable to fulfill that desire until she moved to South Carolina.

After her move to Moncks Corner, South Carolina, she attempted to get her life back on track and was finally able to rent a house. Coincidentally, Anna's sister occasionally attended the Catholic Church in nearby Summerville, and she called our church one day to ask for her sister Anna to be put on our church's prayer chain. I was praying for Anna long before I ever met her!

Meanwhile, my husband was sponsoring someone into the church and, while at RCIA one day, Anna appeared. She had no car, so my husband gave her a ride home after class. He told me about her, and I had this huge nudge from Jesus that I should go to the next RCIA meeting and offer to sponsor her if she wanted me to. I did attend. I met Anna and was immediately drawn to her and liked her. At the end of the class, I offered to be her sponsor. With tear-filled eyes, she eagerly exclaimed, "Yes, thank you so much!"

We gradually became friends. I began picking her up every Wednesday for our RCIA class and every Sunday for church. This continued for four months, and with each trip, our friendship grew. The first night I met her, while getting to know her, I talked about my Cursillo work. Anna immediately exclaimed, "I want to go!"

I laughed and replied, "We have to get you Catholic first!"

Being a convert myself, during RCIA I was able to notice when she really didn't understand something in class. On the way home, I would take time to explain it to her. This opened the door to many faith discussions. All the while, our friendship grew. I introduced her to many of my Cursillo friends, invited her to gatherings at my house and to grouping with my Cursillo friends, and I arranged for her to attend Ultreya for three months.

Her family was very happy about her new life and began spending time with her. She was overjoyed. After every RCIA class, she would call her daughter and tell her what she had learned. Her daughter, a Baptist, was questioning some things about her own church. Who knows what might happen there?

Anna joined the church at the Easter Vigil. What a beautiful service! Five of her family members came. Right before she was confirmed, she whispered to me, "I'm almost a Catholic!" When she went to receive her first Eucharist, the priest had the three candidates relight the candles that they had lit at the beginning of the mass. As Anna approached the priest, he said something to her about the light coming into her life. It was so special. When Anna sat down she said, "Now, I AM a real Catholic!"

Three weeks after being initiated into the Catholic Church, Anna was on her way to her Cursillo weekend. Anna has multiple health issues, and I was very concerned about her being able to physically endure the entire Cursillo weekend, so I had many people praying for her. I insisted that she take her oxygen with her. I was working team, so I was there to keep an eye on her. On Friday night of the weekend, after supper, she did not feel well, so we put her to bed with her oxygen. I was worried she might have to go home. Many of us prayed for her. Anna awoke the next morning and was fine for the rest of the weekend. God is good!

The thing that amazes me about this story is that the whole time I've been trying to help Anna, she has turned around and helped others!

Once, I obtained some gift cards to Piggly Wiggly from the church. I gave them to Anna. The next time I saw her, she said, "I hope you are not going to be mad at me, but I gave one of the cards to someone who needed it worse than I did." Another time I took some Christmas things to her that I was going to give to the Salvation Army. She took a few things and then asked me if I would take her to the homeless shelter where she had lived, so she could give the rest of the things to them. She has a heart of gold, and it is obvious that the ripple effect is at work here. I started out to touch Anna's heart, but she has touched my heart and that of others even more. As always, you receive more than you give when you are doing the Lord's work.

Great things happen when God mixes with us. The power of prayer is awesome. As Eduardo, the founder of the Cursillo movement tells us, we must always be looking for the faraway and bring them into the light. Anna came from the dark into the light and sprouted into a beautiful flower. I made a friend, I became a friend, and I brought that friend to Christ!

MY REFLECTION ____

____

____

Faith Tested
Andrea Marcella

How often our faith is tested!! A few months ago, I was faced with a hard decision about whether to leave my job as an assistant to the activity director at an assisted living facility or retire for the fourth time. I was afraid that if I retired, I'd become bored, and I would feel useless.

You see, I've been working outside the home most of my adult life in one capacity or another. I guess I was letting my various jobs define who I was. I prayed about it for a couple of months before I finally made the decision to retire. I put my faith in Christ, and I can tell you, I haven't been bored or felt useless. Christ has been showing me the plans he has for me and been putting me to work!

Now I have time to do more for our church through working with the Women's Guild. One of the services we provide is a meal after a funeral. This is a time to offer ourselves to a family who is hurting and in need of comfort and prayer. What better way to be community to those in need? Live your faith.

MY REFLECTION ____

____

____

Chapter Seven
Actual Grace

Actual Grace Summary
Deacon Coleman Parks

God is constantly inviting us into intimacy with Him. He created all of us because He wanted to share His life with us. As you start to understand that you are going to experience a whole new meaning to life, peace, joy, and an awakening that only comes from God filling your innermost self with His all-sufficient Grace. Grace is an undeserved "Gift" from God that allows us to become the adopted children of God. It's an invitation to enter a new or deeper relationship with Him.

If Habitual Grace, as we learned earlier, is the outpouring of God's love into our lives, God's sharing of His divine life with us, then Actual Grace is an even greater outpouring. It is frequently supplied by God at specific times when we need it for a particular reason. It is a kick in the pants, a nudge, one that provides us with the ability "to do what God does." It is Actual Grace that allows God to work through us in the normality of our daily lives.

The more we accept His Grace, the more we see our faith mature. Faith, when coupled with prayer, will allow us to recognize Actual Grace when it occurs in our daily lives. We start trusting more, are strengthened to resist sin, and we acquire a greater willingness and desire to witness and share the many gifts we have found in God's generosity. All this is Actual Grace.

When I left my Catholic high school and headed off to college, I thought I didn't really need God's help and fell into indifference to God, an existence that acknowledged God but had no time or need for Him. Because of that poor decision, my life became a struggle to hold on to any kind of lasting happiness. I was not alone. I saw a lot of emptiness in others my age as we all tried to fill that void with everything but God.

God was, at best, someone I only called upon when I was in trouble.

Shortly after graduating, a lot of my friends were getting married, and I thought that would be a good solution for my life, too. I married a Baptist girl, and I got dunked in the big tank at First Baptist Church. Still, there was no close relationship with God, nor was God in my marriage. Four years later, I was divorced and a single father. It would be this little baby, who depended on me for everything, who would help me understand I, too, was dependent, dependent on my Father in heaven.

Once again I started to make God a daily part of my life. As soon as I returned to God, He started pouring His amazing Grace upon me... and I started living His plan for me. I remembered the importance of praying, talking to God, and I headed back to my Catholic faith. God's Grace got a hold of me and everything started getting better. My life. My job. My relationship with Him. Then He really set me on the right track. He sent me a good Catholic woman full of Grace, and 36 years later, she's still the best Grace God ever gifted me. Actual Grace.

A lot of people have seen God. Adam and Eve, according to our Bible, only heard God, but Moses saw God. Mary and Joseph saw God. All the disciples saw Him, and the fact is, we have "SEEN" Him as well. We have seen Him in many different ways. Most often it's in an experience, an awareness of something that we know only God could have done. It might have been a solitary feeling, like watching a beautiful sunrise, seeing the stars in the sky, or watching bluebirds fledge from their nest and take their first flight. What about the human body - the complexity and perfection of the DNA chain? That can only be the language of God. What about the birth of a child? I have never experienced anything like seeing my dear wife in labor, and this tiny baby emerging from the womb. It made me realize how **significant** every human life is. For in the birth of a child, we not only SEE God's handiwork, but we participate with God Himself in this very act of

Creation. There is no greater gift than life except eternal life. This gift of life is Actual Grace.

If we are to understand the importance and effect of having a close relationship with God, we must have a clear understanding of what Grace is, and how it affects what we choose to do. We must clearly understand the relationship between Grace and free will.

Both St. Thomas and St. Augustin maintain that Grace is intrinsically and by its very nature efficacious, meaning that Grace can have the desired effect of helping us make good choices, or perform good works. One problem exists. God has also given us a free will choice to either accept that Grace or deny it. We've seen this characterized many times as the little devil sitting on one shoulder and the little angel on the other. It is God's Grace that helps us listen to the little angel. When we listen to God's Grace, we can perform a myriad number of good works. Grace can and should direct ALL our actions.

The surest sign of God's divine life working in us is the presence of His Holy Spirit, first given at Baptism. Yes, in Baptism we are forgiven of sin – both original and actual. Yes, in Baptism we are made children of God. Yes, in Baptism we receive a seal that shows that we are God's special possession. But in Baptism, we are also anointed priests, prophets, and kings. As priestly people, it is our responsibility to give praise to God and to offer Him our worship. It is through these practices that we learn to recognize and receive Actual Grace.

We fulfill our love and responsibility to God when we come to church, participate worthily in the Mass, read our Bibles, celebrate the Sacraments, pray in groups, tithe, and offer simple expressions of praise throughout the day. All these acts acknowledge that God is the center of our lives. By your presence at your weekend, you made God the most important thing in your life. You were right where God wanted you to be, and I pray you all experienced that feeling of Actual

Grace and continue to recognize and give gratitude for it in your daily lives as well. De Colores!

MY REFLECTION ____

____

____

A Special Message
Cindy Tavarez

I recently had the amazing opportunity to give an ambo talk about this year of Eucharistic Revival, our parish plans for events, and encouraging parishioners to go to adoration! Often, when I share about my faith, I am moved to tears. I do not like that about myself and wish I could control the faucet a little, but I accept it as one of God's gifts to me. I feel things and my body reacts with tears: happy tears, sad tears, mad tears, overwhelmed tears, spiritual movement tears.

In preparing for my talk, I knew that there was a high probability that I would cry. I texted many friends and asked for prayers for God's words to flow through me and to NOT cry! Well, I guess it was God's will for me to cry at 3 of the 5 masses. I even cried at the Spanish Mass!

Spanish! Yes, I can speak broken Spanish. I am far from fluent and the last time I read Spanish was back in high school. I had no plans to cover the Spanish Mass until I was reminded of it as we went to a graduation party for a Hispanic youth group member after the Saturday evening Mass. My husband was doing the homily at the Spanish Mass the next day and was not going to be available to help me. My friend called on me to check to see how my Saturday evening Mass talk went.

I was proud to announce I did not cry! She was so proud of me and gave me a lecture to stop saying negative things about having to give ambo talks. She claims that I do an excellent job, and I need to accept that I do it well. I was thankful for her encouragement; however, I was panicking because I had not thought to ask someone to speak at the Spanish mass! She gave me some names and told me to call them for help right away!

Well, after hearing her tell me how great I was and building up my confidence, I decided I was going to trust God and that He would make a way for me to do this talk in Spanish! I used an online translator and practiced a few times. I was struggling with a few words and thought…my son has a Spanish minor! Without much thought to what I was asking my son to read, I asked for his help with the translation and if everything flowed well. He gave me a few pointers and helped me with some words, and I was feeling like I could actually do this! Surely, I wouldn't really understand what I was reading and would not cry. Well, when I tell you it was a miracle, it was a surreal event that I will not forget. I read in Spanish, I understood what I was reading, and relayed the message well. And, yes, I cried.

After the Mass, I was greeted with many smiles, compliments, and beautiful words of thanks for the message in Spanish. I didn't understand a word people said, I would smile and nod. A lady came to me and spoke to me in English and was so thankful for the message as she was also moved to tears. I was humbled at what had just happened and thankful for God's blessing. All I know is that whole weekend was nothing but God working in me and through me. I had prayed for the guidance of the Holy Spirit and Mother Mary, and had recited, "Jesus, I trust in You" before each talk.

While I strove to bring a message of encouragement to the parishioners in our parish, I didn't realize that I, too, needed to hear the message about spending more time in Adoration. I woke up bright-eyed at 6 a.m. on Tuesday, and God reminded me of the opportunity for Adoration that day.

I got ready, and I went to both mass and adoration. Thank you, God, for allowing me to hear and receive the message that I thought was for the parishioners. I was humbled; that special message was for me!

Now, after continuing to ponder on that weekend, it occurs to me that God was working through me in yet one more way. I had asked my son, who struggles with belief in God, to help me with a talk on the Eucharist, the revival, loving Jesus, and going to Adoration. I am thankful that God orchestrated the weekend for those seeds to be planted in him. Perhaps that special message was also, and most importantly, for my son. "Jesus, I trust in You."

MY REFLECTION ____

____

____

The Day I Received Actual Grace
Sharon Shymansky Roberts

I didn't know how to begin, so this story has remained untold for almost four years. I am sitting in my home chapel, and Jesus is right behind me looking over my shoulder. I pray I get this story right and can express to you the flood of indescribable joy that came from this moment, the joy I feel all over again each time I recall it. I pray you will feel my joy as you read this story and that it will help you understand Actual Grace.

First, let me share a little background with you. I had recently made my Cursillo weekend and had been grouping with a reunion group for six months prior. After my weekend, I felt a strong pull to come to know Our Mother. You see, I am not a cradle Catholic, but a Baptist convert. As such, I knew *of* Mary, but I didn't *know* Mary. When I felt this tug to learn more about her, my group recommended I begin by reading Fr. Calloway's book, *No Turning Back.* I did and I was on fire to know more. (I have personally shared with Father Calloway that his book started me on my journey to Jesus through Mary!)

I returned to the group and asked, "What's next?" They told me to read *My Heart Will Triumph*, by Mirjana Soldo, one of the six children who witnessed the first appearance of Mary in Medjugorje. While Father Calloway's book started my journey, this book solidified that Mary was calling me. What do you think they recommended next? If you said *33 Days to Morning Glory* by Michael Gaitley, you would be correct. This group was totally responsible for my heart opening to Our Mother and my consecration to her, but I in no way expected or deserved what happened next.

It was early morning on January 1, 2021. True confession - I hate January first of any year! Something is frightening about it. While I am certain there will be moments of joy and happiness, I am also confident there will be trials and possibly even the death of a loved one. It scares me. On this January first, I rose early and crept through the silent household to our Carolina room. I settled myself into my favorite recliner, pulled the blanket over my legs, and proceeded to pray. I prayed specifically for the strength and courage to face whatever God planned for me in this coming year. I prayed to see His hand in everything and to know that, even in the tragedies that might come, all would be well with my soul.

A few hours later, my husband Dan and I were in our car. I don't exactly remember where we were going, but I do remember what happened during that brief drive. My phone pinged. It said I had a message. At the time, I didn't text. I didn't know what it was, really. I didn't even know my phone had the capacity to send and receive text messages. You can tell how tech-savvy I was! Through God's Grace, I managed to locate the text. Upon reading it, I let out a heartfelt sob loud enough to frighten my husband, who threatened to pull off the road.

"Sharon, are you okay? Do I need to stop the car?" Dan shouted.

"No. Don't stop the car. I'll be okay in a minute," I said in a shaky voice. Taking a deep breath, I silently reread the text.

I hope this doesn't upset you. It's Christmas time and I guess I just want you to know that I have a good life and great parents and friends and it brought me some peace to see you seem to have the same. I understand if I am a secret and am content to stay that way. In case you worried about your daughter born on March 21st, I am absolutely OK and never blamed you a day. I had a wonderful mother I loved and took care of until she passed 5 years ago and now I look after my amazing father. I get to joke around with my loving brother. I'm sure if I had given this more thought, this would be more eloquent, but I just want you to know I'm alive and doing well. Please have a merry Christmas and know that I wish you much peace in the years to come."

Let me explain. 49 years ago, I was an unwed mother. I dearly loved the father of the baby, and I believe he loved me as well. But I was a senior in college, well on my way to receiving my teaching degree. More importantly, I came from an unhappy home. My mom had married young and immediately got pregnant. The marriage did not last, and she returned home with me. We lived in Anacostia in a three-story home that belonged to her parents. In it, my grandparents, Aunt Honey, Uncle Carl, and my great granddad also lived. I lived there until I was about five when my Mom remarried. The three of us moved into a new suburban neighborhood in District Heights, Maryland, and it was there I grew up. Six years later my sister joined the family, and two years after that we welcomed my brother.

Somewhere around that time, our family started falling apart. Loud arguments between Mom and Dad were daily occurrences. Occasionally, flying objects were involved. Name-calling, threats, and verbal abuse were routine. I couldn't help but feel that I was the cause since Mom had made it known she had married my stepdad to give me a home. It was not a match made in heaven by any means. The father of the baby also came from a dysfunctional family, as his father was an abusive alcoholic. Sweetest man in the universe when sober and frightening when drunk; his mother, however, was a saint loved by everyone in the small community.

Eventually, I decided to tell the baby's father that I was pregnant. He offered his support. Not marriage. Not love. Support. In his defense, I was occasionally seeing another young man, who was the brother of a work friend. He had a girlfriend, but he and I enjoyed canoeing together on the river occasionally. The baby's father likely believed I was intimate with the brother. I wasn't, but he never asked.

Regardless, I had already decided history was not going to repeat itself. I was not going to marry anyone just because I needed a home for my baby. I had another plan. Even though my mother insisted on my having an abortion so I could return to school and get on with my life, that was not an option. I found a wonderful obstetrician who became almost like a dad to me. I loved going to see him. He even offered me a job in his practice. He knew how I felt about taking this baby home to my dysfunctional family. It was not going to happen, and neither was abortion. He offered me an opportunity, and I took it. He had a patient who already had a son and they wanted another baby very badly. Unfortunately, after several miscarriages, he told her she needed to stop trying. There would be no more babies for her. He approached her and her husband about the possibility of private adoption. He told them about me. They were excited about the possibility of adding another child to their family! He broached the subject with me, telling me about their situation. He added, "They are a great couple, Sharon. Very stable. Financially well-to-do. Your child will have a perfect family. What do you think?" I felt a great peace come over me. My child would be loved and taken care of. I agreed.

I gave birth to a daughter, and the day after she was born, I was wheelchaired out of the hospital with her in my lap. Just past the entrance, the adopting family's lawyer, I assumed, met us and took my daughter from me. I had to remind myself why I was doing this. I had to concentrate on what her family life would be like at my home. Nonetheless, I cried all the way home while my mother drove.

I did marry the baby's father a year and a half later, and we had over 26 years of a wonderfully happy marriage until he died in 1999. I had graduated from college and had taken my first teaching job. We got married in August, just before school started. But every March 21st for the first several years, I would be alone in my bedroom sobbing for the daughter I had given away. Eventually that stopped as, one by one, I gave birth to three wonderful sons. I stopped thinking about the daughter I gave away. During the time I was pregnant with her, I had knitted her a pink and white baby blanket and written her a letter. In it, I explained why I had given her away. I wanted her to know it wasn't because she wasn't loved; it was because she was loved so much that I wanted the best for her, and the best was something I couldn't give her, not even close. I told her I would never try to find her. That would be selfish of me. If she ever wanted to find me, though, I would welcome her with open arms.

Until that January 1, I never had contact with her and never tried to find her. I was true to my word. Then Mother Mary and Jesus stepped in and gave me a taste of what joy in heaven would feel like! They gave me Actual Grace, unexpected, unasked, and totally undeserving! I had given away His gift to me, and now my heavenly Mother had interceded on my behalf and brought her back! I often wish I could express in words the intense joy that flooded my soul when I read that text. There are no words. I can tell you, though, that I flew to church, sobbing at Mary's feet, thanking her over and over for the gift of Her love and for that of Her Son. I continue to thank them both every day.

I know what you are thinking. What did I do about my daughter? Did I contact her? What happened? Of course, I contacted her! I texted her later that day as soon as I learned how to do it! We texted over the next few days, and then we decided to speak on the phone. What a GREAT conversation we had! She got to ask questions. I gave her answers. She told me about her life. I told her about her Dad and brothers. It wasn't long before we knew we had to meet. She was living in Georgia and I was in South Carolina, just four hours away. I decided I would give myself the best birthday gift ever, and on February 8, just five weeks after our texting began, I hugged my daughter for only the second time in my life! My husband, who was there, said he felt like he was watching a Hallmark movie! I couldn't say it better. It was the closest God moment of my life, for sure! My daughter and I continue to build a friendship, and she is building them with my three sons as well. God's Grace IS Amazing!

MY REFLECTION ____

____

____

The World Series Saved My Life
Marilyn Oberembt

It was Fall, which means World Series time to me. This particular Fall was 1956, and the day was October 8. I was working at Ampco Metal Company in Milwaukee, Wisconsin as a fill-in helper for several departments, but mainly as a steno worker in the same office as the president's secretary. As in many companies at World Series time, we had a baseball pool, and I joined it on a whim, or so I thought. At break time, about 3 o'clock, several of us met in the ladies' room and did some gossiping. While there, we noticed some steam coming from the faucets, but we were not overly concerned.

Going back to the temporary desk in the Expediting Department after the break, I continued with my work. Suddenly, a person stood before me congratulating me on winning the World Series pool, and he gave me some money. I was thrilled! As my purse was at my main desk, I got up to put the money in my purse. My regular office is in a separate section of the building divided by a short hall where the time clock is situated. As I was putting money in my purse, I heard a loud explosion and looked up to see a man in the section I had just come from, sitting at his desk, but the desk was rising in the air! Then, I saw him rapidly descending and, as I watched, I noticed there was no longer any floor! I picked up my purse quickly and ran for the front door of our building. I was the farthest from the door, but the first person out of it!

Others followed, and we ran across the street and watched as many fire trucks and ambulances came to the rescue. The police also came and directed traffic, which was heavy, as it was about time for our day to end. Many people were coming to pick up wives or husbands. My husband was among them. It took some time for these cars to get into the area because of all the emergency vehicles there, but I eventually found him and we went home.

Watching the news that evening, I learned two things. First, the World Series pool game I had just won was the first ever perfect game pitched in the World Series and it was pitched by Don Larson. To this day, it is still the only perfect game pitched in the World Series. Secondly, I learned that the two people I was working with at the time of the explosion were both killed. Had I not won the pool, I would have been sitting there and would likely also have died.

God always has perfect timing. He wasn't finished with me yet. Indeed, this event may have helped propel me into serving Him. Since that time, I have become a Cursillista, joined a group reunion at my church, became both a Eucharistic Minister and a Sacristan, and am a frequent volunteer wherever I am needed. I hope He is seeing my gratitude and my love for Him!

MY REFLECTION ___________________________________

____

____

God Is With Us
Robin Costanzo

I was a special education teacher and taught severely disabled students in an elementary school. As you can imagine, this career path was often challenging. One day, though, I had cause to remember that we are all children of God and that He is with us always.

One of my students was blind, autistic, and severely mentally disabled. He had cortical blindness which meant his eyes were fine but that damage to his brain had caused his blindness. He could only use two words - "chips" to ask for potato chips and "music" to listen to his tape player. He was difficult to work with. We had to sit close to feed him, and he often kicked us. When doing sighted guide walking with him, I would hold his arm and guide him where I wanted him to go. Because I was holding his arm, my arm was close to him, and he would sometimes bite it.

On one hard day my patience with him was completely gone. I was frustrated and angry. He apparently was able to sense my anger because, at one point, he turned his face toward me and said, very clearly, "Jesus loves the little children."

I was shocked to hear him speak words I had never heard him say! And what words he spoke! I was immediately humbled and gently told him, "Those were the only words that could have saved you today, and if Jesus loves you, I can too." I saw Jesus in that child's face for the first time that day. The young man never spoke again.

Several years later he died from a seizure and his parents donated all his organs. His corneas went to someone who was able to see with them though the original child never saw anything with those eyes. Apparently, though, if he was able to know and love Jesus, his heart was working just fine.

MY REFLECTION ____

____

____

Chapter Eight
Piety

Piety Summary
Sharon Shymansky Roberts

It was Friday night. You were tired and hungry for dinner. There was one more talk on the schedule. The rollista entered, you sang, and somewhere along the line you heard the word "Piety." You may have found yourself thinking, "Oh, please God, no. I am way too tired for this heavy a subject," while visions of nuns and priests danced through your head.

During that rollo, you were introduced to THE TRIPOD. Written on the first leg of that 3-legged stool was the word PIETY. The rollista then gave you the names of the other two legs, STUDY and ACTION. Perhaps you decided right then that you didn't like the tripod at all! None of those words were your favorites! But you were tired and hungry, and you couldn't leave the room, so you unexcitedly began to listen.

You understood that this stool, or tripod, represents the balance we need in our spiritual lives, the balance we need to fulfill our Christian baptismal mission. Piety, study, action. It began to make sense. Piety needs to be an important part of our lives as Cursillistas, but what exactly is piety?

Let's begin with what it isn't, as there are false concepts of piety out there. Let's call the first misconception "sanctimonious." Remember Holy José or Holy Hannah? Their Christian actions occur mostly in the church or church groups. They want others to see them serving in the various church ministries, and they believe that they are Christian in their hearts. However, they are concerned with their salvation and often neglect to help others find theirs. It's all about ME. They fail at their God-given mission as they neglect to bring others to Him. They can also be irresponsible, often lacking the maturity to find that balance between family, job, and church commitments.

Then there are the practitioners. Think Mechanical Mikes and Routine Ritas. They practice all the external signs of a faithful Christian. They believe in God, but they don't have a relationship with Him. They are in church every Sunday, not necessarily because they want to grow closer to God and worship and praise Him. They attend because it is what they've always done, and it is expected. They fear if they don't go to church, they will go to Hell, and they know enough to understand they don't want to end up there. They often place conditions on God when they pray, such as THY will be done, but only if it coincides with MY will!

And let's not forget the Pharisees - Pharisaical Phil and Phyllis. These are the most destructive of all, as they are often models of perfection in church, but unethical in their own business dealings. They may have a large crucifix or sculpture of the Last Supper in their office or on their desk, but they don't model Christ in their actions. They do not practice what they preach.

Authentic piety is seeking continuously to grow closer to God. When you are authentically pious, you already have a relationship with Him, and every day you desire to know and love Him more. Every day you wake up thinking, "How can I be more like Christ today?" Every evening you reflect on, "How was I Christ to someone today?"

This relationship has four components: living a life of Christ in Grace, being conscious of your life in Grace, growing in your life of Grace, and sharing your life of Grace. Piety is the direction of one's whole life to God, and we answer this call by knowing, loving, and serving Him.

In a word, Piety is our ideal. This lifestyle of piety has four specific qualities: natural, courageous, strong, and joyful. The authentically pious person is one you are drawn to because of these qualities. They are the kind of people you want to be around. They are strong in faith and courageously speak their faith, and it is immediately obvious that their joy comes from knowing and loving the Lord.

It began to make sense. That tripod could not stand without all three legs – Piety, Study and Action, and while all are equally important for a balanced Christian life, it begins with the desire to know and love the Lord. It begins with Authentic Piety. Without this first leg, the tripod will never stand.

MY REFLECTION _______________________________________

____

____

Let God Be Your Guide
Debbie Allen

My work environment as a real estate agent is always changing. Many days my office is at a restaurant table sharing a meal with clients. I always ask if we can take a moment to bless the food before eating. My clients seem to welcome the blessing, and it sets the tone for our environment. I'll admit, while I always felt comfortable saying Grace with my Catholic friends, it took courage to initiate saying it with strangers. This practice of praying with clients allows me to "bloom where I am planted." Remember that phrase?

I was recently on the phone late one evening with one of my buyers - a cradle Catholic who no longer practices his faith. He was stressing out about his decision to purchase a very expensive home (the most expensive home I had ever sold) and fear and second guessing were consuming him. With the guidance of the Holy Spirit, I assured him that I was there to guide him whether he purchased this home, another home or didn't buy a home at all. I hung up the phone and said a rosary for him, then another rosary, and then a third rosary. I prayed for him, not for me and the sale. Yes, it was a huge one, and the commission would be most welcome, but I truly wanted the best decision for him. So, I asked our Blessed Mother to give him peace about this decision, no matter how it turned out for me.

The next morning, he called me. I confidently picked up the phone knowing whatever his decision, it was the right one. His voice and attitude were much calmer. I shared that I had prayed three rosaries for him the night before. He thanked me for praying for him. How special! His decision? He was buying the house, and he was excited about it! Gone was all his indecision. Thank you, Blessed Mother.

MY REFLECTION ____

____

____

Increased Piety
Sarah Ingram

In my prayer life, I have learned the value of repetition and rhythm. It keeps me focused. It's taken me several years of encouragement from my Cursillista sisters (and finally getting aspiritual director) that's helped me to recognize this and implement it in my prayer life. The ritual of the Mass, the rhythm of rote prayers - it all helps to center my thoughts, my emotions, and my desires on Christ.

With the help of my spiritual advisor, I've finally set up a rhythm of prayer life that is (so far) working for me to continue to grow my relationship with Christ. First, I've been introduced to the idea of praying in rhythm with my breath. A common prayer of this type is called the "Jesus Prayer." The one that currently helps me center on God is this: "To you, O Lord" ... "I lift my soul." I pray this prayer as I breathe throughout the day. "To you, O Lord… I lift my soul. To you, O Lord… I lift my soul."

Each day I try to attend Mass. I am not a morning person, so this can be a big sacrifice for me. I've found that the daily participation and reception of the Eucharist keeps me steady. Weekly, I take an adoration hour at a local parish. This quiet time with our Lord helps me remember that He speaks to me in silence. Be still and know… you know? And every two weeks (or sometimes once each month), I go to confession, even if I don't "feel" like I need it. This rhythm of prayer has helped me to grow my relationship with Christ, to increase my piety. I encourage you to find your own rhythm of piety that works best for you.

MY REFLECTION _______________________________________

____

____

Meditating on the Rosary
Sharon Shymansky Roberts

I started this rosary practice a few years ago, and then stopped it when I joined the daily scriptural rosary group at our church. Today, Tuesday of Holy Week, was my weekly adoration hour. I felt the strong urge to pick up my rosary and recite it as I used to because it always helped me relate to the mysteries. It seemed like Holy Week was a good time to revitalize the practice.

So, what is it? Well, let's begin with the Sorrowful Mysteries. On each bead in each of the Sorrowful Mysteries, rather than recite a scripture and then say the Hail Mary, I announce the mystery first, as always. Then, I think of one word on each bead that could describe how Jesus was feeling during the time represented in the mystery. Let's take the Agony in the Garden. On the first bead, I think the word "distressed" and I ponder why He might have been distressed? Because a trusted friend was about to betray Him for 30 pieces of silver? Because he knew He was about to suffer even more than He already had? Because He wanted to stay but also wanted to be obedient to His Father? Bead 2. I think the word "grieving." Why? Because He was about to leave behind the apostles and friends, most of whom had spent the last three years with Him. They had become very close, and the fully human Jesus was certainly grieving at their upcoming separation. And His mother? How could He leave her? On every bead, in every mystery, I ponder a word that fits His suffering.

Saying the rosary in this way during Holy Week in our small adoration chapel, before the body and blood of Christ, was so impactful and emotional! Tears truly trickled down my face throughout. But my heart? Ahh. My heart was so alive with gratitude and love for my Lord! I will gladly walk beside Him on Good Friday to experience with Him the joy of our Salvation through His Resurrection.

MY REFLECTION _______________________________________

____

____

Bucket List Maker
Sarah Ingram

I am a convert to Catholicism, and I am also a bucket list maker. I have several bucket lists, all arranged by category – some are "events," some are "things to do for family and friends," some are just "things I want to be able to own one day," like have a house and a dog. Soon after Easter, 2010, I remember feeling so on fire for the Lord that I just had to make a "spiritual bucket list." To this day, it is an index card taped to the mirror in my bathroom. My spiritual bucket list is a list of pious practices I want to be able to do authentically and frequently because, for me, they will encourage my relationship with Christ. Some examples from my list are: attending daily Mass, reading the Bible at night, journaling once a week, setting evangelization goals every day, and going to confession once a month.

Like all new resolutions, I thought I would accomplish everything on that list the first day I taped it up. And like all new resolutions, I failed within the first few hours. However, in all these years I have been trying to be a true Christian in the world, I can tell you that I now do go to daily Mass more mornings than I don't, and that I do get to confession once every month, sometimes more than that! I am slowly but surely accomplishing the things I have set out to do, the things that help me to follow God's will. I encourage you to make your own "spiritual bucket list" and use it as a guide to grow your relationship with Christ and His church.

MY REFLECTION ____

____

____

God is Good…All the Time!
Carlos Dorthalina

I was working in the kitchen at a men's Cursillo weekend, which is a wonderful experience as a true servant. It was decided that we would establish a schedule for 24/7 adoration of the most Blessed Sacrament during this 3-day weekend. As a result, we had the Blessed Sacrament exposed in a monstrance in one of our chapels during the entire weekend. In my own parish of St. Mary Help of Christians in Aiken, SC., we've had 24/7 perpetual adoration for over 25 years.

I had taken an adoration hour in the afternoon, prior to the evening meal preparation. This weekend, we had several newly ordained permanent deacons as part of the spiritual team. Of these newly ordained deacons, I had served on many men's teams with two of them. At the time we served together, both had been lay people.

I went to the chapel a few minutes late and, to my surprise, there were three of the newly ordained deacons in the chapel. One, Michael Thompson, was by himself, apparently preparing for some talk or meditation. The other two were toward the back of the room, adoring quietly.

There was a kneeler positioned directly in front of the Blessed Sacrament. I knelt there in front of the Blessed Sacrament for five or ten minutes. Then I sat in a chair within proximity of the Blessed Sacrament, intending to read and say a rosary for the Rollista giving the rollo at that time.

As I recall, I sat silently for a short period, but I was suddenly prompted to stand up! I turned to the three deacons and said, "Jesus wanted me to tell you to trust in Him." I stood there in shock, after saying that, and then earnestly said to the deacons, "I don't know where that came from!" I immediately sat down, somewhat embarrassed by my outburst, but reflecting on its origin. My good friend, Deacon Michael, came close to me and whispered, "That's exactly what I needed to hear." He continued, saying, "Satan was pretending to be Christ, saying that he was disappointed in me, and that I was unredeemable." The other deacons also indicated that they were struggling with their presentations for this weekend, and they needed to hear that as well.

Amazing things happen when you put your faith and trust in our Lord Jesus Christ! As a side note, I was informed by someone that they had heard of a miracle that occurred on that weekend. That really surprised me.

Deacon Michael later shared with me that he used this incident in a rollo and meditation that he gave on several weekends. The Lord continues to lift us up and use us to build his Kingdom. God IS Good, All the Time. De Colores!

MY REFLECTION _______________________________________

____

____

SATURDAY

Who is Jesus to me?
Why does that matter?

Chapter Nine
Person of Christ

The Person of Christ Summary
Deacon Coleman Parks

Lots of good people introduce other people to Jesus Christ every day. And while many of us certainly already know Him, every day He tries to reintroduce Himself to us in a brand-new way. Intimacy with Christ should be the most important and outstanding note in the life of every Christian. And it's not only the memory of Christ we should focus on, but the Living Christ.

It would be impossible to give one title to Jesus Christ for He is the Lord of Life Who transcends both human and Divine existence. The Person of Christ meditation invites one to encounter both the historical and the contemporary Christ.

As in every Cursillo theme, we see the role of the Spirit in facilitating discernment of Truth in the life, death, and Resurrection of Christ. In this short talk, you get a glimpse of the undeniable distinctiveness of the role of the Son and the Spirit which ultimately leads one to a clearer understanding of Who our Trinitarian God is and ever shall be.

(John 14:7 In-Context) Jesus answered, "I am the way and the truth and the life. No one comes to the Father except through me. If you really know Me, you will know my Father as well. From now on, you do know Him and have seen Him."

The theme acknowledges both the simplicity and significance of the short human life of Jesus Christ, the heralding names the Prophets and authors of the Bible called Him, and the amazing life of this son of a carpenter who was most certainly God made man.

The process is to move the Cursillista from the historical life force of Christ to a better understanding of today's Living Christ, the Risen Christ who emerged from the tomb, and how we all are called to be active participants in that "Living" Christology.

MY REFLECTION ____

____

____

Love Conquers All
Sharon Thomas

I'm sure you are familiar with the scripture in Matthew's Gospel that says, "If you have the faith of a mustard seed, you can move a mountain."

Many of you are mothers. Mothers are very important leaders. They greatly influence their children. Let me repeat that! Mothers are very important leaders. They greatly influence their children. Children start out very cute, cuddly, precious, and adorable. Then they become teenagers.

I remember feeling that I was a terrible mother when my son, Johnny, became a teenager. I tried everything I could to get along with him and finally, I concluded that the only thing left was to pray. So, I began getting up 15 minutes earlier each day to start my day with prayer. Jesus and I had many conversations. St. Monica became my favorite saint. She prayed for St. Augustine, and I prayed for Johnny.

Seven years later my daughter became a teenager! She was a little different than Johnny. She had to have only name-brand things, ordered the most expensive item on the menu and, of course, only ate a little of it, and continually mentioned that I didn't know anything! At least I knew to pray for her.

Well, many years have passed, and with age comes wisdom! Now our children have children and when we get together with them, my husband and I have decided that we have a pretty awesome family. Once we let Jesus be a part of our struggles, we were able to influence our children to become compassionate, loving people.

Johnny often calls me to pray for a friend or client of his. He always says that he has told the person that his mother has a direct line with God. Do you think he remembers those mornings he saw me praying?

The following is a description of middle school-age children that someone gave me. I thought it was perfect!

During the summer before entering middle school, they suffer brain damage and forget much of what they have learned. They wiggle, squirm, stretch and yawn. They tap their pencils, tap their feet or maybe their neighbors and they love noise. They cough, belch on demand, and make other disgusting sounds as a social activity. They sweat, smell, and wear dirty clothes. They sometimes don't like each other, often won't like you, and frequently don't even like themselves. They should all be named Frank because they are. "Your clothes are totally gross!" "Your hairdo is weird!" and, of course, "You are at least 95 years old!" are frequent comments.

They are lovable, they are tenderhearted, they will cry, and they will sometimes want you to hug them, but for goodness' sake, don't let anyone see!

Let me tell you the story about my profession as a teacher. In college, I loved studying to be a teacher and was so excited when I started my student teaching. Whoops! Reality! My cooperating teacher is NOT a joyful person. On the first day, she informed me to look at her desk and notice where everything was and be sure that I kept it that way, because it was her desk and not mine. At lunch, she sat with her friends and told me to sit somewhere else. She was impossible to please! That natural quality of warmth seemed to be missing. I tried and tried, using all my skills to get her to like something I did. Nothing seemed to work. I would cry every morning before I went to school.

Finally, my friends went to the college supervisor and told her what was going on. The college supervisor appeared the next day and took me out of the situation. So, I started my teaching career on probation with a resume from my cooperating teacher that said <u>I had no warmth</u> or rapport with children and was intellectually incapable of teaching all subject matter. My college supervisor said that there would be only one in a million people who would want to be a teacher after an experience like that, but I was that one!

Yes, it was a very humbling experience, starting out on probation. I could have had the attitude of poor me, but instead, I took the initiative to use my gifts of creativity, drama, and puppetry to teach for mastery. I discovered much joy in touching the hearts of children. I especially loved the little challenging boys. I think my experience of my less-than-Christian cooperating teacher taught me what it was like to not feel loved. I worked hard to be sure my students felt loved and helped them to become the best they could be. I believe God gives us lessons to teach us important things about life.

After several years I began praying for my students. During the summer before the start of a school year, I would pray for my new students. On the first day of summer, I would pray for student number 1 on my class list for the next year. The next day was number 2 and so forth. This inviting Jesus to be involved in my teaching had amazing results since Christ and I are an overwhelming majority.

One of my favorite stories of influencing children happened one Christmas. Ian was helping his mother decorate the house for Christmas. He found a music box with Mary, Joseph, and baby Jesus on top of it. He said, "Mom, we have got to give this to Mrs. Thomas for her Christmas present because she loves Jesus."

His mom asked, "How do you know that?"

He said, "Oh, Mom, when someone loves Jesus you just know!"

Davonte, one of my former first-grade students is someone I will never forget. He appeared one day from New York. His mother had been on drugs, and he was now living with a guardian aunt. While I was teaching, it was not uncommon for him to be parading around the room singing, "Yankee Doodle went to town riding on a pony!" If the class was sitting in a circle, he would stand right in front of me to get my attention. In the hallway, it was always Davonte and Mrs. Thomas holding hands at the front of the line and then the rest of the class behind us.

These disruptive behaviors went on for four months until I could work through the red tape to get him on medicine. One day at lunch, Davonte asked me to teach him to pray. I told him to close his eyes, fold his hands, and talk to God. He said he didn't know what to say. I told him to say whatever was on his mind. With his eyes closed ever so tightly, and his hands folded, he said, "Dear God, please help me to be good for Mrs. Thomas." I thought it was the best prayer I had ever heard. I was showing a bit of initiative, one of those natural qualities we talked about earlier, since we were in a noisy public-school cafeteria praying! I had fallen in love with Davonte. The other children loved him, too. It was like they sensed that they should treat him like I did. They were patient, kind, and understanding with him. I often felt that Jesus was in the room with us.

Davonte did not leave my side all day. He had a special chair next to my rocking chair. Sometimes he would move his desk by me, and he would always sit next to me at lunch. However, when it was someone's birthday, he would tell the birthday person that because it was their special day, they could hold my hand in the hallway and he would walk right behind us.

When Davonte was first in my class, the other teachers used to pass me in the hall and whisper, "I'm praying for you," with the look of *I'm glad it's you and not me*! But after a while, they passed us and smiled. I know that Davonte and I were visible symbols of love in the school, and we were the topics of many conversations. I believe we were influencing them.

When people asked me how I had been able to turn a "little terror" into someone so loving, I would say that I just looked for the good in him, as I knew he was a child of God. I was able to convert a seemingly unbearable situation into a wonderful adventure through love. Isn't this what Jesus is asking us to do - spread love to all corners of the world?

I'm sure you have all heard, "My yoke is easy and my burden light!" I don't think I understood this for a long time until recently. A yoke is a wooden bar by which two animals are joined at the heads or necks to work together. So, if we think of being yoked to Jesus, we realize that, in difficult times, Jesus is there helping us to handle anything.

Not long ago, I was visiting my best friend from high school. She gave me a yoke that her father had used as a sheep herder. I have it on the wall of my porch and every time I walk by it I am reminded of being yoked to Jesus.

MY REFLECTION ____

____

____

Being Christ for Others
Sister Mary Frances Epplin

At the beginning of the pandemic, our Community reduced the lay staff to essentials (health care, kitchen, building maintenance). Since March 2020, I have been serving each day at the Reception Desk. Among the blessings of my assignment is the opportunity to meet a variety of people -- believers and "nones."

I encounter our Savior Jesus in each person whether receiving prayer requests, welcoming physicians and physical therapists, media reporters, chaplains, internet technicians, truckers, appliance repair teams, young women discerning their vocation, language teachers, chapel organ tuners, funeral directors, plumbers, benefactors... Each person in my day minsters to me as well, and I desire, with God's grace, to be Christ's hands, ears, eyes, and speech for them.

Most mornings, *Geoffrey* calls the Front Desk of our Motherhouse to learn the "saint of the day." After I open the switchboard, I consult our devotional book *In Caelo et in Terra: 365 Days with the Saints* to share an inspirational reflection with Geoffrey, who struggles with depression and anxiety. Grateful for his 32 years of sobriety, Geoffrey hopes to learn the trade of a barber. At the end of our conversation, we turn to our Mother of Guadalupe and pray a *Hail Mary*.

Gregory, an evangelical Christian, called from Los Angeles. Our Sisters sponsored a showing of *Sound of Freedom*, and he brought his wife to the phone. Together we prayed the Lord's Prayer for children trapped in human trafficking and for young people in gangs on the streets of their city.

Gina frequently calls from New Jersey. Afflicted with agoraphobia and physical disabilities, Gina seeks encouragement through her illness. Gina's 80-year-old mother has been battling cancer for over three years. Gina's social worker suggested that they "fill their lives with beautiful music." Gina is building a collection of *Spotify* recordings by the Daughters of St Paul choir: *Handmaiden of the Lord, On Wings of Peace, Sing Your Praise*, and *Christmas Favorites*. We often speak about lifting up our suffering to the Heart of Jesus, praying "Jesus! Jesus!" And "Mother Mary!" Gina also welcomes a reminder to open the windows to absorb the sunshine and fresh morning breeze.

A few weeks ago, **Kathleen** called from Maine. "God put into my heart... to renew Eucharistic adoration," she confided. As a nurse assistant, Kathleen shared her "complicated faith journey." Recently, during a Visit to the Blessed Sacrament, she sensed the Heart of Christ suspended over the sacred monstrance, "growing and glowing." She felt a call to be an apostle of the Internet, "overcoming the dark forces of evil." She will suggest and supply pamphlets and devotional books from our *Pauline Books and Media* webstore.

Rose, from Indiana, was recommended by her pastor to write her experiences as a pro-life advocate in a "Witness to Life book." As a professional puppeteer, she wants to do "something special for God." She was delighted to learn about our *Dare to Dwell* podcasts.

This summer **Diane** called from Indiana. She manages a bookshop in a university town and invites passers-by with window displays, author events, book clubs, and prayer groups. For the Eucharistic Year, she is preparing a DVD on the Real Presence with resources from our Publishing House.

Mark, a professor, displays papal documents published by our Sisters in the "trophy" cabinet outside his office. This is one way that Mark reaches out in Evangelization to the college students and faculty.

Yes, God is good, for each day I encounter Him repeatedly in every voice, in every face He sends my way.

____

____

Bringing Friends to Christ – It Can Happen Anywhere!
Bill Thomas

I was teaching sixth-grade math in a public school when we got a new sixth-grade science teacher. Finally, there was another man in the sixth-grade hall! For a long while, I had been the sole man among fourteen women! Greg was former military and, like me, had gone back to school to become certified to teach. I was assigned as his mentor to help him learn the ropes and to help him complete his initial evaluation. Along with the fact that we had a lot in common, and we had to work together on evaluation, we were now the only 2 men with fourteen women. We ended up spending our planning periods together working on evaluation stuff. Greg was a good guy, and we quickly became friends. We talked about our families, our interests, the women teachers, and, as soldiers often did on 2 am military security watches, we talked about religion. Greg, an active member of a big, non-denominational congregation, and I, a "Cursillistafied" Catholic, had some wide differences... but many points of agreement as well. Most importantly, we both were interested in growing in our faith.

After several weeks, the faith part of our discussion began to dominate our time, and we wanted to start a teacher prayer group. We chose the friendliest of the women and asked her to join us. Lynn said yes, and after our first session, she asked if Barbara could join us, too... and then there were four!

We met one day each week for about ten minutes before class started. Soon, other teachers noticed and, when they learned what we were doing, they asked to join. By January, the entire sixth-grade hall would meet in my room every Tuesday for ten minutes before the kids came in. We brought petitions for ourselves, our families, friends, students, etc. This continued for two years.

Then Greg moved to Alaska and had to leave the group. Alaska was too far away to allow Greg to attend our prayer group and still get back to his class on time. His replacement, thankfully, was another man. His room was next to Barbara's, and she was the first to talk to him. She rushed into my room one morning all upset. "Bill, you have to do something! I invited Matt to join our prayer group, but he said he was an atheist!" Guess who we prayed for that week?

Now our group was only 15 teachers - 14 women and me in my room every Tuesday. I would step into the hall at 7:48 and whistle and the women would hurry in. They referred to themselves as Bill's harem. Others outside of our teacher group began to notice. One day one of my students, after seeing us through the window, asked what we were doing. When I explained it was a prayer group, she asked if she could join. Of course, that would not be allowed in a public school. I told her we would pray for her. After that, she would sometimes ask for our prayers when she had a test coming up or some other need.

Over the years, we prayed up several miracles. One of Lynn's students was diagnosed with a degenerative spine disease and the doctors put a rod in her back. We prayed for her for the entire year and when she was in for a checkup doctors found that the spine was regenerating. They could not explain that. The regrowth was so complete that they removed the rod and she regained normal flexibility.

Matt, the atheist, was a good guy, and even without the religious connection, we became friends, although not close like Greg and I had been. However, as we talked about our "histories," he related some family stories that helped me understand why he had rejected God. I tried to help him see God was not to blame. I hadn't yet changed his mind. . . but I saw that he began to relax his anger.

We continued our prayer group until I was transferred to the seventh grade. I was in a different building then, so I couldn't continue with the group. The sixth grade continued the prayer group, however. I tried to start a group in seventh grade. The scheduling was different, and it worked for a while with a few teachers, but it didn't last. We didn't have a friendship base to build on.

All in all, the experience was a good one and bore fruit. My wife started a prayer group at her school. A Cursillista friend heard my story and started his own environmental group at his work, and Lynn and I started a Friday evening Bible study group with our spouses and several non-teacher friends. We were Catholics, Methodists, and Presbyterians and all focused on improving our relationship with Christ. Bringing friends to Christ can happen anywhere, no matter in which square meter you are planted.

MY REFLECTION ______________________________________

____

____

Answer Aggravation with Kindness
Sister Mary Frances Epplin

A few years ago, I was working on a committee with a woman who criticized everything I suggested. She would put me down and was for<u>ever</u> sending me <u>disturbing e-mails</u>.

I must admit, I was really tempted to <u>retaliate</u>. If you could have seen some of the e-mails I was composing in my head, <u>it would curl your hair</u>! But I kept telling myself, that I am a Daughter of St. Paul and, to be <u>true to who I am,</u> I must respond with <u>Christ's charity</u>.

I prayed about the situation and felt the grace to bring her before God in prayer—asking for the blessings <u>she needed</u>. I also recognized that my tone of voice and carelessness were aggravating our strained relationship. Gradually I realized that I could <u>relate </u>to her, not with anger, but with <u>kindness</u>. And before long, the irritating e-mails stopped coming!

This kind of self-encounter can happen at any time—but will seldom appear in the <u>headlines</u>!

MY REFLECTION ____

____

____

Chapter 10
Study

Study Summary
Tommy Smith

Saturday morning of the weekend took on a new kind of energy. You probably remember feeling more comfortable with your fellow candidates as well as seeing that God had something in store for you as the day kicked off. There was the beginning of a sense that things were connecting, and all this was going somewhere. And bang, the first Rollo of the day smelled suspiciously like work.

The Rollista announced that this rollo was on the dreaded "S" word - STUDY! You thought you heard a collective "Ouch! "Or perhaps you heard, "No, not me! I don't like to study or read." But, since no one left the room, you were stuck there on a precious Saturday morning listening to one of your least favorite subjects.

Yes, that was the prelude, but what you learned was critical to that entire day. Looking back, you could see the day was about the Person of Jesus Christ and who He should be to us. This rollo centered the day. The key phase of the Study rollo was, "You cannot love what you do not know." The process of studying about Jesus, though, starts with us. Who we are and what are our strengths and weaknesses? What has been our life experience so far? Do we have a relationship with Jesus, or have we neglected Him.? What should our attitude be about Jesus? All of this requires reflection and, yes, study. Another element of the rollo was a discussion about tools we can use to learn about ourselves and about Jesus. The list, of course, started with the Bible and The Catechism (Bible and Catechism in a year, anyone?), spiritual books, spiritual direction, podcasts, websites, prayer time, and Eucharistic adoration to name just a few. We learned that without this second leg of the tripod, piety and action will not work either.

What became evident was that, for us to grow in our love and understanding of Our Lord and Savior Jesus Christ, we would need to grow in our *desire* to know and appreciate Jesus. We would need to grow in our *desire* to understand ourselves and the specific role He has for us. We would need to grow in our *desire* to know and develop our knowledge of our faith and the Catholic Church. This entire package of Study will be an ongoing journey for the rest of our lives, but the reward will be an overflowing love for Jesus and an incredible gratitude for being alive and chosen to follow Him.

Study, then, is the natural outgrowth of focusing on Jesus in our Piety since we now want to know more about Jesus. And, Study anchors the third leg of the tripod, Action, since loving Jesus means we want to do His work in the world to change it to Him. Wow, all that from the dreaded "S" word, Study!

MY REFLECTION ____

____

____

My Metanoia
Sharon Thomas

I would like to share with you my metanoia. You may remember that metanoia means "the change in one's way of life resulting from penitence or a spiritual conversion." Metanoia is often a progressive thing.

Mine began when I was three and was baptized in a Presbyterian Church. At that time, the only emotion I felt was ANNOYANCE that my dress got wet! I had no idea that the Holy Spirit had entered my being. Now, through study, I realize what a comforting friend I was given on that day. It was the Holy Spirit who has been guiding me to live a Christian life ever since.

When I was in grade school, my best friend was a Catholic. One day she told me that she wasn't supposed to play with me because she was Catholic, and I wasn't. We decided to not pay any attention to that rule!

During high school I went to church every Sunday and was active in the youth group. I had a group of friends, and we did lots of things together. One of those friends wanted to become a priest, and every Christmas we would all attend midnight mass at the Catholic Church. It was beautiful, but I did not have a clue what was going on.

While going to college, I attended church every Sunday with my roommate. We attended the Methodist Church. I prided myself on being a very ecumenical person and was pleased that I felt comfortable in any church.

My Lutheran Granny had told me that she would disown me if I ever married a Catholic. This presented a problem when I fell in love with a Catholic man. Thankfully, after she got to know "Mr. Wonderful," she dropped the subject. We were married in my church with my minister and a Catholic Priest officiating. It was an extremely ecumenical wedding since Bill's mom was Catholic, his dad was a Mormon, my mom was Baptist, and my dad was Lutheran. We used the Jewish candle lighting service during the ceremony. I figured we had everything covered as to what the correct religion was! Everyone came and had a great time.

My husband, however, did not feel like he had been to church when he went to the Presbyterian Church with me, and I did not want to go to a different church from my husband. So, I attended the Catholic Church with my husband every Sunday. After 13 years, I joined the church. I went through RCI A, but I really didn't understand all the rituals. I was comfortable with my own religion, and I didn't want to open my mind to anything new.

Then, I went to my Cursillo weekend. When I sat where you sat, I couldn't wait to get home, get signed up for team and give a talk! Now, let me tell you, giving a talk involves – study! There is an outline to follow, scriptures to look up, and suggested books to read for background for the talk. ENTER METANOIA! I started studying, reading Scripture, devouring religious books, and listening to religious CDs.

You could say I was a slow learner! I have been in Cursillo for over 35 years and have heard the same topics you heard on your weekend about 50 times. However, there were always different religious and laypeople giving the talks, and I continually came away from a Cursillo hearing something "earth shattering" that I had never heard before. The more I studied the Bible, the passages that I thought I knew, became more alive for me. Through the understanding of the rituals of the Catholic Church, mass has become a beautiful, meaningful experience.

As a result, I am learning how wonderful Jesus really is, because you cannot love what you do not know.

MY REFLECTION ____

____

____

By the Grace of God
Mike Motta

We are all broken and scarred in some way. Some more than others. Honestly, I didn't realize how true this was until I attended my

Cursillo weekend (Men's Weekend #78, Columbia, SC). Getting to know my Cursillo brothers, and hearing their stories, illustrated that brokenness.

My journey began in 1994. I had just completed college when I was hired to work for a company in Wichita, KS. While in Wichita as a single guy, I met many people, including my neighbor who was a Filipino and a devout Catholic. She introduced me to many more Philippine folks and, before I knew it, I was invited to birthday parties, Christmas gatherings, and all kinds of get-togethers. Eventually, I became a regular and familiar face within the Philippine community of 200+ people.

As I became more established in the community, I met a young lady with whom I became very fond. Her mother and father were born in the Philippines and came to Wichita, KS to practice medicine. Her father was an OBGYN and her mother was a Doctor of Psychology. As it turned out, her Dad was very deep into the Cursillo movement, having been a rector several times. He was also heavily involved in the Kansas State Ultreya and the National Cursillo Encounter. None of that meant anything to me at the time. Again, this is in the mid-90s. Back in the mid-90s, as I have recently learned, the Cursillo movement had gained momentum in the US, particularly throughout the Midwest – 40 years after the first US Cursillo in Waco, TX in 1957. As I got to know him and his family more, he began encouraging me to do a Men's Cursillo Weekend. For whatever reason, I wasn't ready at that time, yet that was my first introduction to Cursillo. The year was 1995.

Years passed. The young lady and I had ended our relationship, and by 1999, I had moved back to my home state of NJ, still without having made a Cursillo weekend. Looking back, I believe in my heart it was not the right time. The right time for me was just a few months ago, in February 2023. Here's why…

Although I had been strong in my faith during the mid to late 90s, that quickly faded as my priorities shifted from the church to the things I now know are only temporary highs - money, popularity, and materialistic things. For the next 15-17 years, I allowed myself to chase those things that, today, give me little satisfaction and happiness. Most importantly, it is clearer to me today that these superficial things are not sustainable. They can be taken from us at any moment, and I learned that the hard way.

Both my parents are second-generation Italians, so I'm a cradle Catholic. In my family, that meant nothing more than showing up late on Sunday morning at mass (just before the Gospel!) and leaving immediately after receiving holy communion. My father prided himself in getting a jump on the traffic by leaving the parking lot early. We never stayed for the end of mass. Unlike her son, my grandmother was the typical little old Italian lady with the black veil. She had an unofficially assigned seat at every Sunday morning mass, and conversation with her was off-limits for the first 60 minutes of every day so she could say her prayers and a rosary. Unfortunately, I was two generations away from growing up in a committed Catholic environment. As I look back, we were just checking boxes. I grew up with a father who didn't realize his example-setting wasn't exactly that of a man of faith.

From childhood through my senior year in high school, I attended mass with my parents maybe 50% of the time. During my five years of college, I attended mass only occasionally until a pretty little girl caught my eye one weekend. Then my mass attendance went up to 80%! After college, as I mentioned earlier, I moved to Wichita, KS, and my mass attendance stayed consistent at about 70%.

My company moved me to England in January of 2000, where I spent the next 4 ½ years. This is where the wheels began to fall off. I stopped going to church and practicing my faith. Not because I stopped believing, but because I was more focused on the superficial things I mentioned earlier.

In an old historic Catholic Church in England in the year 2003, I married a girl from Ukraine. That event was the first time I had been in church in 3 years. I would not attend mass again until late 2008 when my twin children were baptized. From my children's baptism to 2013 (when the kids made their first holy communion at Corpus Christi in Lexington), I was not particularly good at attending mass regularly. My priorities were all wrong.

Well, it all changed for me in 2020 when, for the first time in my 30-year career, I lost my job. Almost immediately after, my wife walked out of the marriage. I was out of work for seven months. During Covid, companies in my field weren't hiring. Both life-changing events happened within four months of each other. Maybe you can relate to this. Maybe you have had similar challenges, and you know what it's like to be at your absolute lowest. The one redeeming quality for me is that I don't drink very much, and I never did drugs, never even tried drugs at any time in my life. So, I suppose things could have taken a major turn for the worse had I taken that fork in the road like many do. The devil was very tempting during that time.

Then my life turned around. About two years ago, I woke up one Sunday morning (still jobless) and found myself four rows from the last pew on the Mary side of our church. Deacon James Chin was serving mass that day. I remember it like it was just yesterday. (*Incidentally, nine months later, it was Deacon James who first approached me about attending Cursillo. Things happen for a reason!*) I didn't know one soul in the church that morning. I was alone, with no friends or family, but I didn't feel alone if that makes sense. Every time I look back at that day, for the life of me I cannot remember getting out of bed, taking a shower, getting dressed, or driving myself to church. All I remember is opening my eyes and the very next thing I have any recollection of is sitting in church at 8:00 mass that Sunday morning. For the longest time, I couldn't explain it. Today, I honestly believe it was the Holy Spirit who was guiding my movements that day.

Fast-forward to the summer of 2022, when Deacon James cornered me at hospitality one Sunday morning. He and I had met a bunch of times since that first mass I attended. In his not-so-subtle way, he said, "We have a Men's Cursillo Weekend coming up. You should attend!" If I remember correctly, my response was, "Are you Filipino?" It brought back fond memories from my days in Wichita and spending time in the presence of a certain Filipino doctor who lit up as bright as the sun every time he spoke about Cursillo.

I had a calendar conflict with the very next Cursillo weekend. Deacon and I, however, stayed close on the subject over the next several months. He eventually connected me with Mike Weinzapfel, who mentored me through the program. My confidence in Mike quickly faded when he wouldn't commit to picking me up Sunday night after the Cursillo weekend. On the car ride to Our Lady of the Hills, I asked him 3 times, "What time are you picking me up Sunday night?" He wouldn't answer me! I thought for sure he was going to drop me off and never pick me up!

Everyone I spoke to about Cursillo before my weekend said the same thing, "It will change your life forever." Well, I like to think I'm experienced enough to NOT be easily convinced when someone says something is going to change your life. During the six months between Deacon talking to me that first time and the Men's Cursillo weekend #78, I had lots of emotions. For starters, I had extremely lofty expectations. But I was also anxious, skeptical, and a little nervous. With all that being said, I was also very much looking forward to the weekend.

Because of my Wichita experience, and multiple conversations with Deacon James, Mike Weinzapfel, and eventually Mike Bozzo, my expectations were super high. I was at a challenging time in my life, and I was looking for answers. I desperately wanted a personal relationship with God. I wanted to hear and see the signs that people talked about. I wanted God to guide me in every decision I made. At this phase of my life, I had decided to stop chasing money and material things. When I consistently started back at church two years ago *(and have NOT missed one single Sunday mass or holy day of obligation since)*, I glanced in the review mirror at all the things that had made me feel good over the years, and what I saw were nothing but temporary highs and unsustainable joys.

To my surprise, the Cursillo movement HAS changed my life. It's not just the weekend – it's everything connected to the movement: weekly grouping, Ultreya, being on team for the next Men's weekend (#79), and most importantly, the friendships and the Cursillo family that I'm blessed to be part of. While my outlook on life and the new path I wanted to take was already going through a makeover, Cursillo became the vehicle that opened my eyes to recognize what's truly important and what's not.

Where did that drive for unsustainable joys come from? Well, taking you back to my childhood once more, my dad is a guy who grew up in Jersey City, NJ and never finished high school. There was no money in my family those days. He was an underaged Navy enlistee during the Korean War. He came out after four years and drove a truck for a while, then became a toll collector on the NJ turnpike, and eventually became a full-time firefighter. He retired after thirty-two years of service.

His advice to me growing up, in my mind, was very short-sighted. I didn't know that then; I do now. "Find a job that makes lots of money. Money buys happiness." Maybe his advice comes on the heels of growing up without much money. Most Italians came to America with nothing. Nonetheless, that was his advice. "Go make a lot of money and you'll be happy." So, that's what I did. I chased the good life. I don't think I was a bad person along the way. I was always very respectful and kind to people, and I never drank too much or did drugs. My addiction was climbing the corporate ladder and making lots of money. I never took care of the important things in my life, most importantly, my faith and my love for Christ. Understanding this today is important to me because I know now, unlike the materialistic things I chased for so long, my faith and Christ's love for me are the only things that can NEVER be taken away.

The Cursillo weekend changed the way I view the world and our purpose here on earth. Unfortunately, it took two major life-changing events to get me here. But I'm finally here, and I like where I'm at. Cursillo is very emotional for me (I say "is" – present tense – because it continues to have a deep spiritual impact on me every day). *As an Italian, my emotions are on steroids anyway!* But, between the Cursillo weekend, the monthly Ultreya meetings, and the weekly grouping with the all-star team I'm fortunate to be part of, I now feel the Holy Spirit regularly. Admittedly, I get frustrated sometimes when I don't feel Him all the time. But coming from a time in my life when I never recognized the signs (or refused to recognize the signs), I now let Him guide me every day. In Mathew Kelly's book, *Rediscovering Catholicism*, Kelly emphasizes the need to repeatedly ask Christ, "What should I do?" I do that now and I have learned to pray for big decisions. These days the Good Lord speaks to me, and He's answering my prayers and guiding me every day.

Cursillo certainly continues to help me personally, but one thing I have not mentioned yet is how it's helped me better understand the need to help our neighbors. Maybe it's easy for me to think this way now that I've been through some life-changing challenges. But it's opened my eyes to understand how many people need our help. How many people struggle every day with family issues, job issues, sicknesses, addictions, etc.? It's our job to help. I'm not looking to take credit for anything. I'm not looking to be recognized. I'd rather see virtuous deeds be done in secret. (Matthew 6:2-4 So when you give to the needy, don't announce it with trumpets…when you give to the needy, don't let your left hand know what your right hand is doing, so that your giving may be in secret). Please don't take this next part as if I'm looking for credit. I mention these things just to help you understand how Cursillo has changed me.

Today, I find the need to give back and help. For example, about 5 months ago I started volunteering for 4-5 hours a week at Chapin We Care (food pantry). I'm also an officer with Our Lady of the Sacred Heart Knights of Columbus Council in Chapin and a 4th degree Knight with the Bishop of England Assembly in Columbia. This is a fraternity founded in 1882 and today has more than 2 million members worldwide and 16,000+ councils across the globe. It's supported by four key principles: Charity, Unity, Fraternity, and Patriotism. These four principles touch me in every way, but it's Charity that has the most impact on me. Our Catholic faith teaches us to "Love thy neighbor as thyself." Members of the Knights of Columbus show love for their neighbors through numerous ways of serving our parishes and communities. For instance, these include things such as conducting food drives to support local food pantries such as the We Care food pantry, volunteering at Special Olympics (such as Columbia Screaming Eagles special needs children, providing "Coats for Kids," and aiding victims of natural disasters and other catastrophic events, local and worldwide. For example, since the Russian/Ukraine war broke, the Knights created the *Ukraine Solidarity Fund* and, to date, we've donated over $21M from 60,000 donors, 220,000 care packages, 60,000 rosaries, and 6.9 million pounds of supplies to Ukraine. That's the kind of stuff that gets me excited. I'm also part of the Men's Club, a group that does quite a bit of fundraising specifically for our parish. But all this, in my mind, is never enough. There are still people in need, there are sick people, lots of people still have addictions, folks are homeless and jobless, etc. We can always do more…

In summary, I am more convinced today than ever that things happen for a reason. I lost my job and my wife within four months of each other. My life, leading up to that point, was off the rails. I was heading down a path leading away from God. I wasn't recognizing the signs that we need to guide us toward a life of Christ. I was NOT taking care of what matters – my faith in Jesus Christ. And as mad as I was at the time, I truly believe today, in my heart, losing my job and the disruption to my family life at the same time was the Holy Spirit grabbing hold and knocking some sense into me, and pointing me toward the path I should have taken twenty-five years ago. Recognizing how lucky I am today, I still ask myself daily, "Why should I be so lucky that Christ chose to save me when so many people in this world need help?" I was saved for a reason. Maybe it's because He chose me to do his work here on earth, helping others.

I like being on the right path. I like the Holy Spirit making my decisions. I like helping people in need. It feels good to have an intimate relationship with the Good Lord. I owe my 180-degree turnaround to Jesus Christ for not giving up on me and guiding me to mass that unexplained Sunday morning two years ago. And I owe those of you (especially Deacon James) who not only encouraged me to join Cursillo but who walk side-by-side with me every day on this journey. After having committed to the Cursillo movement, I now recognize the Holy Spirit is with me every day, and I am thankful for that. I put my faith and trust in Christ, and I commit my life to serving Him and serving others. I am thankful to be living a *Life of Christ* today. De Colores!

Sandy
Wendy Borowy

I met Sandy in the summer of 2022. It was at our community water aerobics class on a Thursday morning. I was already in the pool, water up to my neck, hiding my imperfections! She hurried in wearing a naturally infectious smile and a very tasteful, bathing suit, that fit exactly how the designer intended!! I wondered, "Will we be friends?"

I could tell right away that she was humble and kind. I was amazed that she offered to teach swim lessons to one of our classmate's two grandchildren for two weeks. Her patience, sweet prompting and encouragement motivated them. She did it just because she had the time, and because she enjoyed it!! I wondered, "Do I have enough ENERGY to be her friend?"

I didn't run into Sandy for many months after water aerobics. It was at this year's Advent Mission at my church, Precious Blood Of Christ. She lit up as she saw me exiting the church. As usual, I knew the face but couldn't place her or remember her name! I remember wondering, "Where do I know her from?" Then I received a Divine Prompting! "Talk to her, she's one of you girls!" Of course, she lived on my street! We were in water aerobics together! Now I remember.

She said that had been looking for a church to call home and was led to attend this Catholic Church. She already had a deep love for Jesus and a growing devotion to our Divine Mother. She told me she wanted to know more about the Church. So I showed her around, in and out of the Church. I explained the Adoration Chapel, the Tabernacle, and why the Eucharist is the center of the Catholic Church. I wondered, "Am I being too pushy with this holy bombardment?"

She was joyfully taking it all in and wanted to know more! So, I took the opportunity and invited her to our prayer group! We officially call ourselves Our Lady of South Carolina Prayer Warriors! A few of us girls were Divinely placed in each other's lives and called to pray together for our families, friends, Holy Mother Church, our nation and all the world.

Our format is simple, yet powerful. We call it MARY 9-1-1:

9 Memorares

1 Holy Rosary

1 Divine Mercy Chaplet

We pray in front of the tabernacle or in the side church chapel every Wednesday. We share our faith with each other, bringing new devotions, prayers, information; all to aid in our loving and praising God. Our holy discussions have been life-changing! Sandy accepted our invitation, making us 6 strong at that count! (We are now 7!) I wonder, "Who will be next?"

For Sandy, this new Catholic life was like jumping in when playing jump rope, "1,2,3 jump in!" She was in at "1"!! Just in time for the Lenten Week Mission!! She attended all the masses and talks given by Sr. Briege McKenna and Fr Pablo Escriva. When not at the church, she participated as a true member of the group attending lunch with our famous guests, a Southern tea, a Rosary walk at the beach, and a Faith-filled day at Our Lady of Joyful Hope SC Shrine in Kingstree.

Sandy continues to go to mass every day and is a true Prayer Warrior! In addition, her knowledge about the Saints is mind boggling to me! She has read the entire Diary of St Faustina, writings of St Theresa of Avila and her favorite, St John of the Cross! I would dare to say, most

Catholics, have not read those books!! I wonder, "Will she decide to become a Catholic?"

She, also, is a true and loving friend. She listens with a compassionate ear and shares her love of Jesus. Recently, I told her I was worried that my son would go to Hell. He had told me years ago that he didn't care about going there as long as he was living his way. She started to cry, saying "No, no, no, don't ever say that! Jesus has him! Have faith!" Her reaction was pure, motherly love. She knew my faith had been shaken. She reminded me of Jesus's love and mercy! She was right. I wonder, "WHEN is she going to become Catholic?"

She loves the Bible verse, John 15:5- "I am the vine, you are the branches. If you remain in me and I in you, you will bear much fruit, apart from me you can do nothing". That sums up her Faith. That sums up the Catholic Christian Faith as well! She has gifted me one of her most cherished devotional books, "Jesus Calling". On March 30, the daily reading focuses on Trusting Jesus. It says, "Search for me as for hidden treasure. I will be found by you."

As I write this I am thrilled! Finally, Jesus has called her to be a Catholic! She has enrolled in the PBOC RCIA Program to be brought into the church at the Easter Vigil, March 30, 2024. I am honored to be her sponsor!! Jesus called her and she said "Yes!!"

Now I wonder, "When will she become a Cursillista?!!"

MY REFLECTION____

____

____

Chapter Eleven
Sacraments

Sacraments Summary
Deacon Robert Pierce

This is a subject at the heart of the life of the Church, and thus at the heart of our lives as Christians. What is it that makes the Church so essential for our ability to live rightly, to understand why we are here at all, and, in the final analysis, to be truly happy? Let me ask it another way. What kept Abraham, Isaac, and Jacob going? What kept Moses and the Israelites going in the desert? What kept David and his descendants going? What kept the Jews, even when in exile, going? THE PROMISE.

And how did God ratify those promises? He formed covenants with the people. How did he seal those covenants? With an oath. To Abraham and Moses and David, he said, "I swear by myself." When Jesus died on the Cross, God said in the most powerful way possible, "I swear by myself." The Church is the keeper and the protector and the guarantor of God's promises today. What are the promises, the covenants, the oaths that God gives us through the Church? The SACRAMENTS.

The Sacraments constantly remind us of the mystery of God's plan for mankind. However, mystery is not a truth we cannot understand. Rather, it is a truth so vast and deep that we can only grasp a small portion of it. This little glimpse into the sacraments is to whet your appetite for this immense treasure so that you might experience this mystery with greater love and devotion.

There are many definitions of a sacrament, each conveying the same essential aspects. One I like is: "A sacrament is an outward sign of an inward reality instituted by Christ and given to the Church to communicate His life to us." Each Sacrament has outward signs we recognize through our senses like water, oil, chrism, bread, wine, words, etc. These outward signs communicate an inward reality as God fulfills His covenant within us. There are seven Sacraments for this simple reason: Jesus gave seven Sacraments to the Church. The Church did not invent them; she only defines and defends them. We receive grace in each Sacrament because we encounter and receive Christ in them.

The Sacraments touch all the stages and all the important moments of the Christian life: birth (Baptism), maturing (Confirmation), strengthening by food, drink, and table fellowship (Eucharist), repair and restoration (Penance), service of others (Matrimony and Holy Orders), and strengthening in serious illness or preparation for death (Anointing of the Sick).

Man needed no Sacraments before The Fall because he had a face-to-face intimacy with God. Similarly, we will need no Sacraments in heaven. Our fallen human nature needs them now because each Sacrament is designed in some way to 1) heal sin and bring us closer to God, 2) restore our lost innocence, and 3) bring about our future perfection.

Pope Benedict XVI wrote that creation exists to be a place for the covenant that God wants to make with man. The goal of creation is the covenant, the love story between God and man. Only when man is in covenant with God does he become truly free. We know that Jesus came to further convey to man that creation exists to be a place for the covenant that God wants to make with man, to continue and deepen the love story. The covenant between God and man is established and ratified through a series of oaths. Just as God said to Abraham "I swear by myself," so also in the Sacraments.

But how can we know <u>for sure</u> that God will be there? The major events of your life are so important that Jesus raised them to the dignity of Sacraments so that you could be assured of His presence throughout your lives. A covenant involves an oath – in Latin, a *sacramentum* – the word from which we derive the word "sacrament."

Each Sacrament involves an oath, but not an oath *by us*. Rather, it is God who swears the oath. Please understand this important point. God participates in the covenant. In Baptism we hear, "This is my beloved son." In Confirmation, "Receive the gift of the Holy Spirit." In the Eucharist, "This is my Body. This is my Blood, the blood of the new and everlasting covenant." As it says in the scripture when referring to marriage, "What **God** has joined, let no man separate." Each aspect of our Christian lives is so important that not only do we take a vow but, more importantly, God swears an oath to help us, to give us His grace if we make Him a partner in our lives. That is how we can know that God will be there to help us.

<u>This is why the Sacraments are one of the greatest spiritual treasures that the Church offers to all and makes available to all Catholics.</u> In each Sacrament, we are given a particular sacramental grace that corresponds to what we are called to be, that corresponds to the mystery in which we participate. Whether we <u>feel</u> it or not, Christ has promised to be there. Will we let Him in?

At the center of the sacramental life of the Church is the Eucharist. How does the Church see the Eucharist? The answer is packed into Canon Law, Paragraph 897. It is worth reflecting upon in your prayer time. "The most august Sacrament is the Most Holy Eucharist in which Christ the Lord himself is contained, offered, and received and by which the Church continually lives and grows. The Eucharistic Sacrifice, the memorial of the death and resurrection of the Lord, in which the sacrifice of the Cross is perpetuated through the ages is the summit and source of all worship and Christian life, which signifies and affects the unity of the people of God and brings about the building up of the body of Christ. Indeed, the other Sacraments and all the ecclesiastical works of the apostolate are closely connected with the Most Holy Eucharist and ordered to it."

There is no way to overstate the importance of the Eucharist. Even Canon 897 understates it. The Sacraments are the crown of the Catholic faith, and the Eucharist is the crown jewel of the Sacraments because the God we believe in the Creeds and obey in the commandments, we meet and receive in the Sacraments, most completely in the Eucharist. The desire for a loving union between God and man is achieved most perfectly in this life in the Eucharist. This is love's ultimate end - union. A deep, interpersonal union is God's desire, which will find its fulfillment in Heaven. The Eucharist is the most intimate union between us and Christ that exists in this world.

Everything in the Church, especially each of the other Sacraments, is ordered toward the reception of the Eucharist. The Eucharist is God, the fullness of Jesus' humanity and divinity, among us. That is why the Eucharist is the source and summit of the Christian life, and why it is the center and epitome of our worship. However, where does it fall in our individual lives?

God made promises to Abraham. God made promises to Moses. God made promises to David. God made promises to the Jews through the prophets. When Jesus died on the Cross, God said in the most powerful way possible, "I swear by myself." Each of the Sacraments makes actual that promise in ways unique to the circumstances of our lives.

This is INCREDIBLE news! I only hope that you get some glimmer of an understanding of what our Faith and what the Sacraments are all about. I hope that you recognize that what you need, and what you might possibly be missing in your life, are here for you. And it's backed by a promise that can never be broken.

MY REFLECTION ____

____

____

JMJ
Sheen Jones

For ten-plus years, I was an extraordinary minister of Communion to the homebound and those in senior and nursing facilities. I loved it. When the COVID shutdown came, all EM activity ceased. After two years, I was starting to doubt if I would ever return to this ministry. I was even toying with the idea of asking for my name to be removed from the parish list of homebound ministers.

Then I attended Cursillo #77 in September 2022. It was like a shot in the arm to my faith life. I don't think I consciously decided to return to this ministry, but when the parish office called to ask if I would be willing to take Communion to a parishioner who was no longer able to get to Mass, I immediately said yes. Talk about bringing Christ to others! This ministry allows me to literally do just that. And except for my own Communion times and spending time in Adoration, I never feel closer to Jesus than when I am carrying Him in a pyx next to my heart. The drive from church to my communicant's home is a special alone time with Jesus and me in the car, no music, no radio. I can choose to talk to Him, or I can choose to just enjoy His presence. Either way, this is special "Jesus Time" for me.

MY REFLECTION ___________________________________

____

____

The Power of Prayer in Christian Community
Paula Belken

When I was a Cub Scout den leader, I became acquainted with the father of one of my scouts. I learned that he was a single parent. His wife had abandoned him and their three children. He was an Air Force pilot and was required to be away from home for days at a time. He had hired a nanny through an agency, but she was rather young and overwhelmed with the responsibility of managing a household and three children. The children were dealing with grief over the absence of their mother and were not bonding with the nanny.

I began praying for the whole family. I asked God to use me in some way to help them. Since all three children were involved in extra-curricular activities, it often meant that the nanny had a very tight schedule in transporting them wherever they needed to be. It occurred to me that I could offer transportation to and from Cub Scouts. While this took a small part of the burden from her, she still felt that she could not manage the responsibilities and she resigned. To make matters worse, the father was due for a ten-day trip out of town and had no one to stay with the children. I had four children of my own and no place to put three more. I felt helpless and could only imagine what he was going through.

At daily Mass one morning the reading was from the second chapter of Sirach. I felt that this reading would speak peace to his heart. The next time I saw him I told him about the reading. He asked me to email it to him, so I sent the reading as well as the Psalm for the day. I decided to submit a prayer request over the Cursillo network. I briefly explained the situation and purposely left out names. I just asked everyone to pray that the right person would come into his life to care for him and his children so he could have peace of mind to do his job to support them.

The most amazing thing happened! At the school carnival, he approached me with a beaming smile and said, "Thank you." Bewildered, I asked him why. It seems he had started dating someone who worked for a deacon at the diocesan office. The deacon happened to be a Cursillista who received the prayer request. The deacon printed it out and handed it to his coworker and said, "This sounds a lot like the guy you are dating." She read the prayer request and replied that surely it must be him. She then showed it to the man she was dating and asked if the prayer request was about him. He recognized my name on the email and exclaimed "Yes!"

God wanted both of them to experience first-hand the love of Christian Community and the awesome power of prayer. His need for prayer had traveled through the hearts and lips of over 100 prayer warriors to Heaven, and evidence of that prayer was placed right in his hands! God did answer those prayers. The man found a wonderful new nanny with just the right balance of love and discipline to bond with the children.

MY REFLECTION ____

____

____

The Body of Jesus
Kim Gotz

When I was a young girl, my grandmother and my great-aunt took me to their Catholic church Mass with them one Sunday. We were in Connecticut visiting my aunt. I was Protestant at the time and about thirteen years old, I believe. Just before the time for receiving Communion, I asked if I could receive. My grandmother gave me a firm. **"NO!** You are not Catholic!" However, my Aunt Lucy, shushed her and told her that Jesus would never deny himself to the little children and that it was not my fault I was not Catholic. She leaned over and told me how to hold my hands and what to say. She then got a serious but loving look on her face and said, "You do understand that you will be eating what looks like round bread, but IT **IS** THE BODY OF JESUS. Do you understand that?"

I said, "Yes. "

She asked, "Do you BELIEVE it?"

I answered, "If you say it is true, I believe it."

So, I received Communion that day. I did not know it then, but it forever changed the course of my religious life. From that day on, I felt the pull to the Catholic Faith, but my mom and dad did not attend church regularly. I visited Catholic churches after that from time to time and always felt a special "feeling of home" there. My grandmother died when I was twenty-seven. We had moved to South Carolina from New Jersey four years earlier. We went to the only Catholic Church we knew, Immaculate Conception in Goose Creek. On the day of my grandmother's funeral, celebrated by Father Ernest Kennedy, I made the decision to convert to Catholicism. I knew what I felt was a pull to God. I began taking classes not long after but moved midway through to Wisconsin. I continued taking classes there and on April 3, 1999, I was received into Full Communion with the Catholic Church. When I received my Communion that day, the circle was complete. I was where I was supposed to be. I am sure my grandmother and great-aunt were looking down with happiness as they watched from above. My whole religious life began with one taste of the Eucharist, though I was not worthy then. You can imagine it was the *first* thing I confessed during my First Confession! Thank you, Jesus, for never letting my desire to receive YOU diminish.

Side note... I married a Catholic man, and our marriage was convalidated at Immaculate Conception in Goose Creek, where my son was also baptized. The funny thing is, Father Kennedy, the priest who celebrated my grandmother's funeral founded St. Philip Benizi Church in Moncks Corner, SC which is now my home parish and the parish where I currently serve as secretary. The Lord works in mysterious ways!

MY REFLECTION ________________________________

____

____

Miracles and Healing
Katie Reilly Lund

I began feeling poorly October 2nd, 2022, with severe abdominal pain. Despite many phone calls, I couldn't get medical care until October 12th. I was given an antibiotic prescription, but there was no relief from my pain. I couldn't see a gastroenterologist until October 27th, at which time I would only be able to see the PA, who told me to take Miralax. She also set an appointment for me for Dec.15th for a colonoscopy. I began asking my Cursillo group for prayer.

The **first answer to prayer came** when I could not manage the pain any longer and called the hospital for the gastroenterologist on call. The doctor called me right back. I told him my history of diverticulitis and peritonitis in 2004. This was on October 31st. He listened to me and told me he was at the ER, and I should come immediately. In the ER, I was given a CT scan and was told that I had a large mass that was likely cancer. They admitted me.

I received a colonoscopy on the morning of November 1st. While I didn't yet have the result, the gastroenterologist told me it was likely a malignant mass, and he would have me see a surgeon immediately. The surgeon came in that same morning and harshly said, "You have no time to think about this. You have a large mass that is probably malignant, and you have a choice of surgery or Hospice."

I sat up with all my strength and said to him, "Don't say another word to me! You are too harsh! You know nothing about me and could never understand what the word Hospice means to me. I just lost my husband to colon cancer, and I hadn't thought about having cancer myself."

The doctor said, "Listen, I am due for surgery right now. Sometimes, I have to give people bad news, and I don't want to sugarcoat it." I told him his demeanor and approach were totally unacceptable to me, that I believe in God's mercy, and that my God is a loving God. I told him I would speak with my children before I decided. He was stunned by my reaction. After speaking to my children, I let the medical staff caring for me know that I would be prepared for surgery the next morning. I called my prayer team from the Life in the Spirit group and my Contemplative Prayer Group, and I called my Cursillistas.

I believe the **second answer to prayer** came the next morning when my doctor's partner, also a surgeon, came in and said, "Wow, did you shake up my partner! He was so upset when he came back to the office. He admitted he had really mishandled this situation and was completely humbled by your response to him." Later, when the surgeon came to take me down to surgery, I told him I had every prayer team, including the monks at Mepkin Abbey, praying for me and for him as well. His response was, "I don't know much about monks but, if they are praying for me, that is a good thing." This time he was gentle, kind, and reassuring. That was the morning of November 2nd.

I continued my prayers to God our Father, Mary Immaculate, and even to my husband, Bill. My children and I continued to hear about all the prayers being said. I came out of surgery well and was resting in a semi-conscious state when my **third answer to prayer, or maybe my first miracle,** came.

Now, I know the difference between a prayer and a vision. I have been blessed in my life by two other visions in a wide-awake, prayerful state. They were long ago. But this time, I saw and felt my husband Bill walking down the driveway of our long-time home towards our car. He was about thirty-five, and strong and handsome. I had just put my three children in the station wagon to go to visit my parents some distance away. I opened the window, and he leaned in and kissed me saying, "Honey, please be careful, because everything precious to me is in the car with you." I knew that everything precious to him still was because my three adult children, who all live a distance from me, were with me there as I came out of surgery. And I knew that Bill and God were with me as well.

The surgeon removed a large mass, and I had a colostomy in my diverted intestines. I was fine with it and happy to be alive. I was now reciting prayers of thanksgiving. I was quietly and thoughtfully praying that I would be healed. In the coming days, I shared prayers with friends and family and waited, waited, waited for the pathology report. I prayed The Divine Mercy Chaplet and so did many others. Each day the doctor would come in and say that the pathologist needed another day. That went on for over a week. I prayed to God to spare me because my children and grandchildren just lost their father/grandfather. "Please don't take me yet, Lord, but Thy will be done."

Now, being a Contemplative, I have studied much of Thomas Keating, a Trappist monk who brought to the attention of the Catholic community the practice of Centering Prayer, Contemplation. Although I had studied so many of his teachings, I turned on my iPad at 1:00 a.m., as I was unable to sleep and, still negotiating with God, intended to pray The Divine Mercy Chaplet once again. I finally dozed off and **my Miracle began**.

I saw Thomas Keating so clearly. (A dream or a vision, I can't be sure). He said, "You do not need to tell God your story, because He knows it. What you must do is to pray The Prayer of Abandonment by Charles de Foucauld." I woke up quite startled and remembered the name, which was a miracle in itself. I searched on my iPad and found the prayer. I was completely assured, as I offered the prayer, that I was accepting the will of God, and my mind and body rested in complete peace.

At 6:00 a.m., the surgeon's PA awakened me. She excitedly exclaimed, "I'm sorry to wake you, but I have such wonderful news! The pathologist just released his report. THERE IS NO CANCER! There is NO cancer. He cannot find any cancer cells, though he tested the culture over and over!" I praised God and cried tears of joy. My entire circle of prayer partners rejoiced with me.

However, the story continues. On February 21st, 2023, the surgeon performed the planned surgery to reverse the colostomy. Things did not go as anticipated. He could not do the procedure as the intestinal walls were irreparably damaged. I went home a few days later, accepting that I would have the colostomy for life, but I was grateful to be alive.

A few days after I was home, I discovered that my body was leaking fluid from the incisions. I was seriously in trouble. Off to a third surgery I went. It was discovered that a fistula (tear) had happened during my second surgery, and I would have to have the full digestive system closed off to allow for healing.

I suffered through another fifteen-day hospital stay. My eventual homecoming included an IV to accommodate antibiotics for thirty days and a TPN drip for nutrition. I had those IVs for more than two months, which had to be administered by nurses and my children. For nine weeks, one of my children or their spouses sacrificed time and distance from their work and families to minister to me. I had no food or drink for 67 days until we could be sure the digestive system was ready to work. During this time, I had prayers from everyone.

On February 28th, the day after my third surgery I got a call from my dear friend, Sharon Roberts. She knew I was so disappointed in not being able to go to the Precious Blood of Christ Parish Mission to hear and meet with Sr. Briege McKenna, whom I had met years ago. She is a beautiful Irish nun who is well known for her gift of healing prayer given to her by our Lord. Sharon said to me, "Katie, listen to your voicemail." It was the precious brogue of Sr. Briege praying for my healing both to the Precious Savior and to Our Lady, The Immaculate Heart of Mary. I knew that I was going to be healed, but I also knew that it would take a long time and much medical intervention and treatment.

Before I was finally healed, the last doctor who treated me was a wound care specialist. Already boldly telling doctors where I stood, I started by saying, "I trust in my doctors, but I trust more in the Holy Spirit." This doctor smiled and responded, "Especially the day after the feast of Pentecost!" I knew that both the doctor and my God had heard my prayers.

The power of prayer is apparent more in my Cursillo groups than in any other prayer group in my lifetime. The seeking of prayer, asking others for prayer, and giving thanksgiving for answered prayers is a gift that Cursillo gives to its candidates and Cursillistas. I, for one, am extremely grateful!

MY REFLECTION ____

____

____

Chapter Twelve
Action

Action Summary
Neil Fico

Action is the third leg of the Tripod along with Piety and Study. The Piety rollo, which was presented on Friday, clarified what it looks like to have an efficacious prayer life. The Study rollo you heard today, Saturday, talked about getting to know and love God and our Catholic faith by studying your faith, because "You cannot love what you do not know." Thus, Action should be the end product of these first two.

The term "Action" discussed in this presentation refers to Apostolic Action. Apostolic Action is a type of action where a Christian is performing an action directed by the Holy Spirit, to move our fellow brothers and sisters closer to Christ. To better explain and differentiate Apostolic Action from other types of action, let me share some examples. We can perform many types of actions which come from different powers we possess. We can run and jump which comes from our physical power, or we can read and learn which is from our intellectual abilities, or we can laugh and cry with our emotions. These are all examples of action, but they would not be considered Apostolic because they are likely not performed with the intent of bringing others closer to Christ and His Church. Apostolic Action is the expression of our desire to share God's love through action with the intention of growing God's Kingdom here on Earth. In essence, it is "Make a friend, be a friend, and bring that friend to Christ."

How much does Jesus love us? He loves us enough to suffer and die for us on the cross! Jesus's death for our redemption was the ultimate expression of Apostolic Action and, through it, He established God's kingdom here on earth. This expression of God's love for us released the power of his Holy Spirit on earth so we can SHARE in Jesus's divinity.

This is important to understand, so let me explain. The Catechism of the Catholic Church states that GOD created us to KNOW HIM, LOVE HIM, and SERVE HIM in this Life so we can spend eternity with Him in Heaven. We have all been put on this earth by GOD individually to grow in the Knowledge and Love of God and share in His Divine Life. We accomplish this by engaging in a consistent and fruitful prayer life and by studying and learning about God and our Catholic faith.

We are also called to be servants of God in this Life to fulfill this last required step in our salvation. <u>We are called to be Apostolic.</u> What does that mean? The word Apostle is derived from the Greek word "Apostlay," which means "to be sent." When you and I received the sacrament of Confirmation, we were given an outpouring of grace through the Holy Spirit as once granted to the Apostles at Pentecost. This outpouring of the Holy Spirit is a spiritual seal that was given to empower us to go out and preach the Word of God in both speech and action! In truth, we are called to be missionaries! Our mission is to spread the Gospel, or good news, with our actions of love and service. The mission we are sent on is the conversion of this fallen world to Christ. How are we to accomplish this monumental mission? We accomplish this mission by using God's Grace in our ACTIONS, and those actions are best performed within our mantra of "Make a friend. Be a friend. Bring that friend to Christ."

There are many actions that we perform daily that are kind and worthy gestures, but most of these actions wouldn't be considered Apostolic. Let me give you some examples. We can change a flat tire for a person on the side of the road, give a homeless person a couple of bucks at an intersection, or even save a person's life during a medical emergency. Though these acts are good, they may not be accomplishing the mission. There is a component that is missing in most cases, and that component is GOD'S GRACE. If you are not living in a state of grace you cannot build up God's Kingdom here on earth. Simply put, "Grace" is God!

When we are praying, studying, and living a sacramental life in a state of grace, we can be confident the Holy Spirit is going to work in and through us. When God's Grace is working in and through us, this makes our actions righteous and just, which makes our actions APOSTOLIC! But when we are not praying, not studying, and not listening for God's voice, temptation and sin begin to creep in, blocking the flow of God's Grace in and through us, which makes our actions worldly and sinful. As Christians, we are called to be on guard and fight against these temptations! We must, as St Paul says in his letter to Ephesians, "Put on the whole armor of God, so to be able to stand against the wiles of the devil." He said these things knowing we are all going to be tested through the temptation to fall from God's Grace. Knowing we are called to be Apostles of Christ, how do we make sure we can fight these battles and become victorious? By the GRACE OF GOD!!!

The Gospels record the many miracles Jesus performed when he was with His disciples. He cured the sick, fed the 5000, and even raised the dead. While Jesus was performing these miracles, He preached to the people about repentance and forgiveness of their sins. In Mark's Gospel there's the story of the miraculous healing of a paralyzed man lowered through a hole in the roof by his friends to get Him in front of Jesus. The gospel passage says that when Jesus saw the paralyzed man and the faith of his friends, Jesus was moved to heal Him. Jesus spoke to the man saying, "My son, your sins are forgiven," and with that, the man's paralysis left him, and he picked up his mat and walked. To Jesus, it was important that people showed supernatural faith in Him to be healed. We, as Missionary Apostles of Jesus, need to think of our actions in the same way. Jesus performed these miracles so that people would come to believe in Him and repent and turn away from sin. We, as Missionaries of Jesus, are called to feed the hungry, clothe the naked, and minister to the sick. Obviously, not through miracles like Jesus performed, but our actions, like His, should be focused on the spiritual healing of this broken and fallen world. Unlike Jesus, the SON of God, we can't forgive sins and heal people miraculously but, through the graces we receive living a sacramental life, we can live an Apostolic life of Action.

Four elements make actions Apostolic. The four elements are HEAD, WILL, ARMS, and KNEES.

1. HEAD in Apostolic Action is used to intelligently plan our action after giving it proper consideration and reflection.
2. WILL represents when the Actions are performed in line with well-formed judgment.
3. ARMS represent the human part of our actions. After doing the first two elements, we must then execute the action.
4. KNEES are an obvious reference to our prayer life and the sacrifices we offer up.

There are also six qualities that make up Apostolic Action:

1. Be <u>Rational</u> by employing our intelligence to plan out our actions.
2. Be <u>Resolute</u> by making our actions bold, confident, and decisive. When we are doing God's Will, the Holy Spirit will give us the confidence to persevere in difficult tasks.
3. Be <u>Enthusiastic</u>. Be assured, if our action is insincere and not led by the Holy Spirit, we will not be joyful and enthusiastic when we perform it.
4. Be <u>Constant</u>. Think of all who have been praying and sacrificing for you to be here, and many people have performed apostolic activities to put this weekend together.

5. Be <u>Supernatural</u>. Always remember to "Speak to God about our Friend, before speaking to our Friend about God." Without the Holy Spirit being involved in our action, it is simply a kind gesture.
6. Be <u>Apostolic</u>. No problem. If you have done all the above, you will be performing Apostolic Action out of love for God and your neighbor.

MAKE A FRIEND. BE A FRIEND. BRING A FRIEND TO CHRIST! We are called to go out in love and preach the gospel through our words and actions. Just as Jesus sent His Apostles, now he sends you to love and serve your neighbor through APOSTOLIC ACTION!

MY REFLECTION ____

____

____

The Power of Praise
Jimmy Gianotti

I am the lead singer of a contemporary Christian Rock band in Ohio called "The Power of Praise." We sing all over the East Coast, but one of our favorite ministries was singing at Elkton Prison, a Federal Prison in Ohio. Before Covid. We sang there three or four times a year.

We had recently completed one of our Easter "prayerformances" at Elkton. We call them prayerformance" because we don't perform. Rather, we lead in praise and worship with song. Anyway, a couple of us band members were on a Christ Renews His Parish team with our own Parish, St Luke. After the meeting, we were all sharing a close moment with each other. Of course, everyone that was in the band talked about singing at Elkton Prison at Christmas and the Easter prayerformance.

On our renewal team that night was a police officer. He said to us, "You know I think it's great what you guys do, but don't kid yourselves. You're not changing anything. As soon as they get out, they're going to go right back to the life that got them put in there in the first place. The only reason they come to your concert isn't because they suddenly found God; it's because they have nothing else to do in prison. It gets them out of their cells."

Well, when you get to know me better, you'll know I don't keep my mouth shut very often, so I told Ray, the officer, "Ray, I'm not a stupid guy. I know a lot of them are there because they have nothing better to do, and I know most of them will go back to the life of crime, but if we can help change ONE GUY, then all the years we've been doing this will be a success."

Three months later, we went back to Elkton for our summer visit and yes, some of the guys that were there that Christmas night and at Easter were still there. I shared with them my discussion with Ray, and then I told them, "I want YOU to be our ONE GUY. I want YOU to turn from your old life when you get out of here, and I want YOU to live for God!" Every time we are there, after we finish, every single one of them gets in a line and comes up to each of us and shakes our hands. They thank us for caring enough about them to spend our time with them and to help them find God. This time was no different.

I shared the Ray conversation every time we went there after that summer visit - three times a year for the next ten years, I always shared that story. I shared it every single time because we had new inmates every time, and the old ones loved the story, too, so they didn't mind. Every time I would say, "I want YOU to be my ONE GUY," and I would make them sing and dance with us and swear they would be that one guy. Did it make a difference? I didn't know at the time, but I know we planted the seeds.

Wait. I'm not done. I haven't told you about our gift from God. About five years ago, we were playing at the Canfield Fair, a county fair in Ohio, and we pulled a surprisingly good crowd. The audience members were all sitting in front of us on the benches. In the first row to the right, I saw this guy smiling and clapping and praising God. He looked familiar, but we played all over the place, so I wasn't sure who he was. When we took our first break, I went down to thank him for being so into our music, and he called me by my name. That took me back a minute! Where did I know him from? I looked closer at him and he said, "You don't know who I am, do you?"

I replied, "I'm sorry, but no, I don't. You look familiar, though."

He said, "I'm from Buffalo, New York, and I looked at your website and saw you were playing at the Fair, so I drove all the way down from Buffalo just to see you." I looked closer at him and suddenly realized who he was. He had been one of the inmates from Elkton. "You guys have no idea what you did at Elkton," he said emotionally. "A lot of the guys took what you said to heart and turned their lives around. I joined a church in Buffalo and am involved with the church and some of its ministries." Then he gave me a statue of a buffalo and, around its neck, he had attached a little sign that read, "I'm your ONE GUY!"

I looked immediately toward heaven and thanked God for allowing me to see the Harvest. My message to you is to keep doing what you're doing; keep sharing your gifts and sharing God's message in all your environments. Keep living your fourth day, because people ARE watching and listening and, perhaps one day, God will allow YOU to see the Harvest.

Tapestry
Kathy Paxton

One of my favorite pastime activities is doing needlework; this is why I can relate to God through the tapestry analogy. Completing just one piece is extremely time-consuming. The difficulty of completing a piece depends on how detailed you become. The more detailed you are, the more time it takes. God is like that for me; He is in the details of our daily lives and, once looked at in completion, you can see how beautiful His work is. But, sometimes, we only look at the backside of the piece, which can be very messy and give you no clue as to what the actual piece looks like. Knots and strings everywhere! Yet, when you turn it over, you see a beautiful tapestry interwoven with threads of the people we meet.

This reminds me of a waiter my family met on our trip to visit our daughter Colleen and her boyfriend in Boston. On this trip, my husband and I took one of our three grandsons, Harry, with us. The name of our waiter was Kenny. Ironically, his name is the same as our daughter's boyfriend, and this struck me as funny at the time. I knew I would not forget his name (I am notorious for doing that!) At breakfast, he struck up a conversation with us and was very pleasant and friendly. He asked about our trip and why we were in Boston. After some simple pleasantries, he mentioned to my husband John that he must be a Christian since John was wearing a large 3-inch cross around his neck. Kenny remarked that he also was a Christian. We then briefly discussed our faith, and Kenny asked if we could pray for him. We said of course we would. Kenny thought for a long minute and then said he would like prayers for obedience. We then had a brief discussion about obedience, mercy, and faith. Kenny mentioned he would pray for us and, as we left, we shook hands and started our day.

We had a very busy day and, as we were saying prayers that night, John and Harry said their usual prayers. John then asked me if I had any special intentions. I said my intention, and then John said his special intention. Now it is Harry's turn. Harry says, "I would like to pray for our waiter, Kenny, and that special request he had." My heart just melted thinking how my 10-year-old grandson remembered to pray for the waiter and his special request to be more **obedient**.

The next day we got a different waiter but saw Kenny in the restaurant. We then had a brief conversation with him as he passed our table and, as we were leaving, Kenny mentioned we could request him the next time we had breakfast. As we were leaving, I touched his shoulder and said, "You are the light of Christ to the people you serve." He thanked me, and we wished each other a good day.

Since we had forgotten to leave a tip the day before, John went back to the restaurant to leave it for him. As Harry and I were walking out of the hotel gift shop, there was Kenny at the entrance to the restaurant with a big smile and wave for both of us.

On our last day, we requested Kenny and told him about our day and how Harry had prayed for him the night before. Kenny mentioned how we kept him going and staying focused just by sharing the love of Christ with him. We told Kenny how his positive attitude and joy of the Lord made a much-needed difference on our vacation. To witness and share the love of Christ is the best way to start your day, especially with a stranger who soon becomes a friend. We talked about how people can get caught up in the negative emotions of those we encounter daily whether you are vacationing or just trying to serve them. We discussed how, in this world, we need to be people of light, not darkness.

As we were leaving, I again touched Kenny's arm and told him how he lights up with the Joy of Christ. There are some people you encounter who just positively glow with the peace of Christ. He was one of them. You could see it in how he served people and the love he showed through his demeanor, his actions, and how he looked. For me, I wanted to let him know that I could see Christ in his small actions and that the Holy Spirit was filling him with the joy of the Lord. He gave me the biggest smile and said, "Thank you, I needed to hear that."

We left Boston knowing we had just encountered a new friend in Christ. It doesn't matter what Christian denomination others are; we are all brothers and sisters in Christ. When we are open to the Holy Spirit, God will allow us to cross paths with people whom we need to meet and who need to meet us to bring us strength and wisdom to start our day.

Just like the tapestry, our lives are messy when we look at the back but beautifully detailed when we get a glimpse from the front. Each block, no matter how small or different in color, is placed there by God's design. I believe, when we pass away and go to heaven, God will allow us to see the finished product and remind us that, no matter how small each encounter we have on earth may seem to be, each one is there for a purpose and will make for a beautiful design.

MY REFLECTION ____

____

____

Who Fights YOUR Battles
Neil Fico

My wife, Becky, and I had the privilege to attend a talk by Bishop Robert Barron in the fall. For those who might not know who he is, here is a brief synopsis. He is an Auxiliary Bishop of Los Angeles. He manages a large, extremely popular Catholic media organization called Word on FIRE, and he is also a gifted writer, speaker, and apologist.

While visiting our son who was attending West Point, we got to attend a program that Bishop Barron gave to the Cadets and the Catholic Community at West Point. I want to share with you a part of his talk.

Bishop Barron's presentation focused on three soldiers in the Bible: Joshua, Naaman and King David. He shared biblical stories about each soldier. Each of the stories was good, but the story and teaching on King David was the one that really resonated with me and blessed me with a *"great Grace."*

You can find the biblical story of King David in 2 Samuel CH 11. This chapter tells the story of King David, Bathsheba, and her husband Uriah the Hittite. It is, without a doubt, the King's most shameful moment. Let me refresh your memory, as Bishop Barron did for us that day.

It happened in the spring of the year, at the time when kings go out to battle. David the King sent Joab and his servants and all Israel to battle, and they destroyed the people of Ammon and besieged Rabbah. But David remained in Jerusalem. When King David arose from a nap on the palace rooftop, he saw a woman bathing and the woman was incredibly beautiful to behold. The king inquired about the woman and found that the woman was Bathsheba, the daughter of Eliam, the wife of Uriah the Hittite. Then David sent messengers, and took her, and he lay with her, and she returned to her house. And the woman conceived, so she sent a message and told David, "I am with child."

Then David sent a message to Joab, saying, "Send me Uriah, the Hittite." And when Uriah the Hittite had come to David, he asked Uriah how the war prospered and invited him to return to his home. But Uriah did not go down to his house. Instead, he slept at the door of the king's house with all the servants. When David heard that Uriah did not go down to sleep at his house, he invited him back and asked him why.

Uriah answered, "The Ark and Israel and Judah are dwelling in tents, and my lord and Joab are encamped in the open fields."

So, David, invited him to stay longer and had him eat and drink with him and he got Uriah drunk. That night, Uriah slept again with the servants of his lord and did not sleep in his house. So, in the morning, David wrote a letter to Joab and sent it by the hand of Uriah. The letter told Joab to set Uriah in the forefront of the battle, and retreat from him, that "Uriah may be struck down dead." Joab did what King David had asked, and Uriah was struck dead in battle.

Think about it… King David was the person God described as a MAN AFTER HIS OWN HEART, yet even King David was not immune to being tested and falling from Grace.

Then Bishop Barron asked if we could identify the first mistake King David made before he fell from Grace. Can you identify it? He pointed out that King David had other people fighting his battles! The first verse says, "King David remained in Jerusalem, and allowed Joab and all of Israel to fight for him." When? "In the spring, when the kings were supposed to be in battle."

So, why did King David stay back? The Bible does not say. But what is for sure is, if King David had been fighting battles with his men as he had always done in the past, conquering pagan cultures that worshipped idols and sacrificed to false gods, he would have avoided the temptation to sin. He would have avoided his drastic fall from Grace…

Then the Bishop explained WE are no different! He said that all temptation to sin starts when we are not where we are supposed to be, when we allow others to fight our battles. He went on to say that the battlefield is of a supernatural nature, and that we lose our battles when we are not disciplined in prayer and works.

I am sharing this with you to emphasize that we must both pray so we can hear the Holy Spirit prompting us to act, and then act on what the Holy Spirit is prompting us to do!!!

* Bishop Barron is currently, as of July 29, 2022, the ninth bishop of the Diocese of Winona-Rochester in southern Minnesota.

MY REFLECTION _______________________________________

____

____

Chapter Thirteen

Obstacles to Grace

Obstacles to a Life of Grace Summary
Deacon Charles LaRosa

During this talk, it is my hope you will get a better understanding of God's love for each of us. You will understand in your heart that He is forever with us on this earth as we journey to become the best version of ourselves, the individual person He created each of us to be.

That best versions of ourself begins with love. Since it is God's desire to have all people come to the fullness of life in eternal joy, He calls us to the source and being of love … Himself. In John 4:16 we hear, "God is love and whoever lives in God lives in love." In the encyclical titled The Redemptor Hominis, John Paul 2 tells us, "To be the whole person intended by God, one must come to love with the same intensity with which God loves."

The second aspect of becoming the best we can be is life itself. John 10:10, "I have come that you may have life and have it to the full…" This passage affirms the fullness of God's desire for us to become whole and complete in, through, and with Jesus Christ. We are reminded, too, of what is required to have a full life, and that this is strictly ours to live or not live. The promise of eternal salvation: Paul tells us in Romans, "For I am not ashamed of the Gospel. It is the power of God for the salvation of everyone who believes. For in it is revealed the righteousness of God for, as it is written, the one who is righteous by faith will live.

I would like to talk for just a moment about freedom, conscience, and truth. "Freedom" is the power rooted in reason and the will to act or not to act, to do this or that, and to perform deliberate actions on one's own responsibility. By free will, one shapes one's whole life. Human freedom is a force for growth and maturity in truth and goodness. It attains its perfection when it is directed toward God. Every choice is the ultimate responsibility of each individual person. Freedom is not lost when choosing to live by the law of love. It draws us more and more into the freedom of love and loving. That is, living the divine life and becoming the full person desired by God.

Present at the heart of each of us is our moral "conscience." The Catechism of the Catholic Church says conscience "is a judgment of reason whereby the human person recognizes the moral quality of a concrete act that he or she is going to perform, is in the process of performing, or has already completed." A person is obligated to follow faithfully what they know to be right or wrong. Therefore, there is no justification for the phrase, "The devil made me do it." If I can apply that statement to a life choice, then I have already heard my conscience and have chosen to turn from the good for which it is meant.

There is no better scriptural reference concerning "truth" than in the account of Jesus's final discourse found in John's Gospel. "I am the way and the truth and the life. No one comes to the Father except through me. Consecrate them in truth. Your word is truth." But now, let us talk about the elephant in the room, sin. Besides our own egos, which are contributors, the biggest obstacle to Grace is sin. Sin is an offense against reason, truth, and right conscience. It is a failure in genuine love for God and neighbor. It wounds the nature of man and injures human solidarity. The CCC defines it as "an offense against God." In Psalms 51:4, sin sets itself against God's love for us and turns our hearts away from it. Like the first sin, it is disobedience, a revolt against God through the will to become like God. Sin is thus love of oneself even to the contempt of God.

Let us quickly review the types of sin. Mortal sin, the most grievous, destroys charity in the heart by a grave violation of God's law. It turns us away from God. To commit mortal sin, three conditions must exist: grave matter, committed with full knowledge, and committed with deliberate intent. Venial sin is the most common. It offends and weakens charity, though it does not deprive the sinner of Sanctifying Grace, friendship with God, or charity and eternal happiness. Lastly, there are the seven deadly sins: pride, avarice, envy, sloth, wrath, lust, and gluttony. They are called deadly because they readily lead to other sins, sins that can become habitual and can easily conquer the will.

Thus, the first obstacle to Grace is us when we freely choose the things of the world even as we seek the oneness of God. An example might be allowing ourselves to be controlled by schedules and calendars and maybe just penciling God in on Sunday. Another obstacle happens when God is shelved, and laws are rewritten to fit individual needs. Think how often this is happening now in our world and in our own country. Cyberspace, though a true gift when used wisely, can become, through misuse, a source of death in our own time, often destroying body and soul. The last obstacle to Grace, but by no means the least, is the realization that the devil does exist, and he is active. In the Old Testament, there are 85 references to Satan and 170 references in the New Testament, including Jesus's teachings. The CCC tells us we must be clear that we face a spiritual battle each day. Satan didn't leave the world when he was conquered by Christ's death and resurrection. He continues his fight against the love of God's greatest creation, His children. Remember, God has a plan for us, but so does Satan.

How can we overcome these obstacles to Grace? What can we do to continue and deepen our relationship with God? Take heart, there are remedies!

1. The acceptance of Jesus Christ as our Lord and Savior. All we must do to assure ourselves of this is to read John 3:16.

2. We need to acknowledge God's Grace and participate fully

in the Sacramental celebrations that Jesus has given us - Reconciliation and the Eucharist.

3. Study of scriptures and the Church's teachings. Know your faith and defend it through your actions.

4. Regular prayer life. Set up a prayer routine. Find a quiet place where you can invite God into your heart and have a conversation with Him. Go to Adoration, pray the rosary and The Divine Mercy Chaplet.

5. Adorn your home with reminders of God's love - a blessed crucifix, statues, a painting, a beautiful nativity scene.

6. Carry a cross in your pocket and wear a Miraculous medal or any religious medal.

7. Learn the prayer to Saint Michael the Archangel. You are invoking the power of the Angels to come to your rescue when you say it!

There is one extremely powerful and final remedy that is of utmost importance. Frequent and regular contact with other Catholics. Hebrews tells us to meet often to encourage each other. We cannot survive in a world that is hostile and indifferent to Christianity without the support of a genuine Christian community. Remember God's words, "I am with you always, even to the end of the age…"

MY REFLECTION ____

____

____

Before…and After God's Grace
Miguel Garcia-Javier

I am from Veracruz, Mexico, and I am 38 years old. I lived my Cursillo from November 15 to 18, 2018, in Fayetteville, NC. I took the name; St. Francis of Assisi, and I want to share how I have lived my fourth day. First, though, I want to tell you briefly how it was before living my Cursillo.

I was a person immersed in the world, full of grudges. I was an alcoholic. I had a very strong temper, and I did not really know God. I was away from the Church for 20 years, until a person of God invited me to go to God and spoke to me about Cursillo. Of course, it was difficult for me to go because I was a slave to my work, but I encouraged myself to go and made a commitment to the person who invited me. I did not think that by going I would find something that would change my life. I found God. When I left the Cursillo, I left very happy, like most people do, and I was eager to serve God. I began to go to workshops about Cursillo, to Ultreyas, and to friendship meetings. But the enemy gradually began to put obstacles in my way, starting in my workplace, my environment.

I had to work on my alcoholism, my character, and the desire to return to the world that God had already taken me out of. One of the tests was the separation with my ex-partner. I did not understand why things happened, but I left them in the hands of God and His will. Staying alone gave me time to discover prayer and build a more intimate relationship with God. As the years went by, still alone, most of my time was dedicated to the Lord, and I began to love Him more and to know myself better. I discovered I was worth more than I had thought. Soon, though, the enemy began to attack me again. When I felt alone and fell into a depression, at that moment, I remembered that Jesus says in His Word, "Come to me, the tired and burdened." I remembered I had made a promise in front of the Blessed Sacrament during my Cursillo weekend that I would visit him once a week, and I began to do so.

I have made Jesus my best friend and my confidant. To Him, I leave all my problems, anxieties, and needs. What I most longed for was to find a family and, with a lot of faith and kneeling in front of the Blessed Sacrament, I asked that, if it was His Will, would He grant me a family that would value and love me just as I was? I learned to wait patiently because I knew that God's timing is perfect. After two years, the Lord gave me my beautiful family and the joy of being a father, a joy I had not yet experienced. Now I am even happier because I have received the Sacrament of Marriage, and I continue to persevere in my faith. It has not been easy, but with God, everything is possible, and I continue the fight. I attend Mass. I serve the Lord at the Altar as Sacristan. I will continue to go where the Lord needs me until He calls me on my Fifth Day.
De Colores!

MY REFLECTION ____

____

____

Earrings and Books and Supplies, Oh My!
Sharon Thomas

In 1995, I had an experience that involved spreading God's love. I was invited to participate in a teacher delegation to visit schools in Vietnam through the People to People Citizens Ambassador. Program.

When I found out it cost $5000 to do this, I quickly abandoned the idea of going. However, three days later, I felt the Holy Spirit speak to me, and I knew I was going and needed to have faith!

I had made Angel earrings the year before, and my friends had seemed to like them. I decided to make some to see if I could sell them to raise money to fund my trip. SELL THEM?! I HATE TO SELL THINGS! I began making the earrings anyway, working on them daily, sometimes into the early morning hours. People seemed to find out by word of mouth, and they started buying them. I decided to wear the Angel earrings all the time, just because it seemed like a good idea to have Angels close by, and it certainly didn't hurt to advertise my product!

People began stopping me on the street and commenting on my earrings. I would mention that I had some in my purse, and they would buy them right then and there! A couple of businesses donated some money for my trip and, in three months, I had sold 1200 pairs of earrings! Before I knew it, I had $6000 in my account, exactly what I needed plus spending money! MIRACLES DO HAPPEN!

There were 25 teachers on this trip, each from a different state across the United States. We met in California to embark on this experience of a lifetime. When we arrived in Vietnam, all of us were stunned by the poverty of the country and appalled that we did not see one book in any of the schools we visited. Thank goodness each of us had brought gifts and supplies from our schools and communities (about $5000 worth) to leave with these children. I had brought 100 little finger puppets that I had created to teach young children to read. I don't think I have ever experienced gifts so appreciated as the ones we left there.

Just as we had established a Christian community there in the schools of Vietnam in three days, we 25 teachers became a Christian community as well. We arrived with a common mission to spread God's love to the native children in Vietnam and that mission brought us all closer to one another and to Him.

We had many anxieties throughout our trip. One time we were running out of fuel on the airplane and had to make an emergency landing. We all worried constantly about losing our passports and not being able to leave the country. And we experienced a bomb threat on our airplane as we were headed back to the states! We all supported each other through these trying times. When one of the teachers went into hysterics over the bomb threat and was refusing to get on the plane, I told her to go ahead and get on as long as she had on her Angel earrings. She said, "Do you really think they'll protect me?"

I replied, "I don't know about one pair, but I've got a whole bag of them in my purse!" She got on the plane.

We also experienced the joys of being presented with flowers just because we were teachers and, because we were teachers, being showered with an overwhelming outpouring of respect. And who could describe our joy as we looked at the beautiful smiles on those children's faces, smiles that truly melted our hearts. Like at a Cursillo weekend, we used lots of Kleenex and shed many tears of joy as we felt God's love on the other side of the world. It was wonderful to be around so many self-giving individuals. As the song says, "Surely the Presence of the Lord" was in this place. Even though we were all different religions and were in a communist country, God's love flamed the fire of inspiration for all of us. I guess people need people.

Oh, a footnote to my story! Upon returning from my trip, I continued to wear my Angel earrings. No one has ever commented upon them since. I guess God truly does provide for us when we need it!

MY REFLECTION ____

____

____

Amazing Grace
Delmys Yamileth de Mendoza

I am originally from Morazan Yoro, Honduras. I lived my Cursillo #143 from March 28 to 31, 2019, and my group was Our Lady of Fatima.

I am currently married, by the Grace of God, to Arturo Mendoza for 11 years. I had six children, two were born here in South Carolina, and four were born in Honduras. When I was eight months pregnant with my fourth daughter, my partner back then came home one night drunk and on drugs and, while I was sleeping, he stomped on my stomach. I never reported it to anyone, especially my family or the police. However, the abuse was so bad that I lost my daughter, and she never had the opportunity to see the light of day. She was gone.

Here I am trying to serve little by little, because it is not easy, but it is not difficult. I've had ups and downs like any human being. There are times when I no longer want to continue, but I say no, I must keep fighting for what I believe and what I have learned through Cursillo. I have served eight years as Coordinator of Ministers of the Eucharist in my church, Our Lady Star of the Sea in North Myrtle Beach. I was invited by Carmen Beltran to this beautiful course of Christianity and, since then, I am persevering because Christ counts on me, and I count on His Grace. I continue to serve Him daily, but it has not been easy for me. I feel that every time I want to do something, things continue to happen and usually it's a death in the family. It's like something stops me and then I ask God, why me? I question Him. The Holy Spirit has given me the strength to persevere and to think about the Cursillo and what I learned when things happen.

I have had many blessings from God and a lot of sadness, which makes me wonder sometimes, "Why me Lord? Why am I losing a lot of my family that I will never see again?" One Friday night in 2021, on my way to an Ultreya, I found out I had just lost my aunt, my dad's sister. In 2022, I lost another aunt, my mother's sister. I was also on my way to an Ultreya then. In April 2023, I lost my paternal grandfather. On July 14th of this year, while at the School of Leaders, I was told my uncle, my mother's brother, had just died. Lightning took his life. For a long time we have been praying for one of my aunts, my mother's sister, who suffers from leukemia and, eight days ago, another sister of Mom's was diagnosed with cancer. I realize all of these situations are trials and tribulations that God puts in our way, but now I know that He comforts me through the process and gives me strength to go on. As part of my fourth day, I make it part of my witness so that others who may be experiencing the same thing can realize that God never leaves them alone. He is always with us. I have also asked God for forgiveness for questioning Him, and I feel liberated.

I continue to struggle with my fourth day, especially with my youngest son, who now refuses to attend church with us on Sundays, and it becomes a battle. Now, instead of fighting with him, we use wisdom and patience. I also struggle with having my 3rd daughter far away from us to study. It makes me very sad not having her closer, but life goes on and I thank God for the great husband He has given me. Thanks to him, I have been able to get ahead and have a beautiful family together with him. They are part of our humble home.

Despite my sadness, I continue to try to be the best person I can be. I love to help others who are in need. I also love to bring others to church and to speak to them about the marvelous things that God has done in me through Cursillo. Every day of my fourth day, I ask the Holy Spirit to help me convey the message of God. I have realized that sadness does not come from God. I need to be happy because God is in me and with me. This is why I continue to push forward reminding myself that God is my Savior, He loves me, and I know that I can help others get closer to Him. De Colores!

MY REFLECTION _______________________________

____

____

Chapter Fourteen

Leaders

Leaders Summary
Tommy Smith

Saturday had been a long day already. You were eagerly anticipating the last rollo of the day simply because it WAS the last rollo of the day. You mustered up energy by refilling your snack plate and settled back to respectfully listen to the next speaker. He/She did a brief introduction, perhaps, and then you heard the topic of the rollo – LEADERS. Perhaps you instantly shrank in your seat thinking, "Well this is one thing I am not. NOT ME! God surely does not have me in mind when He thinks of a leader." (Or maybe you were among those few who sat up taller, recognizing your leadership skills already and eager to hear yourself described in this talk!)

The rollista introduced the idea that leaders orient and direct those around them to help bring about the Christian formation of society. But the key thoughts laid out in the rollo were – (1) that we are ALL LEADERS because leaders are influencers in their environments, and ALL OF US are influencers in the environments in which we live and work. (2) that Christ and I are an overwhelming majority. Which means, as Christians, we are ALL called to be Leaders for Our Lord! It gets even better. Lay leaders are those who, having heard the call of the Lord, throw themselves decisively into apostolic action. So, Jesus is challenging ALL OF US to be the tools that bring Him into this hurting world.

We learned that, as leaders, we need to develop discipline, warmth, initiative, and generosity. These are natural qualities that are so attractive to others that you do not have to think about leading those around you; you will be leading just by reflecting these virtues. People are thirsting for these beautiful, genuine qualities in others. We also heard that there are supernatural qualities necessary to lead: a vibrant living faith, humility, hope, and love. Look again at the natural and supernatural qualities. Don't you want to be that kind of person? Are you, yet?

So here is the leader's rollo message; Jesus is calling every one of us to be a leader. He wants every one of us, wherever we are, in whatever circumstance we find ourselves, with whoever we are with, to bring it and them to Him. No small task, and we cannot do it alone. That is why we say, "Christ and I are an overwhelming majority."

MY REFLECTION ____

____

____

The Necklace
Sarah Ingram

Last June I quit my job with less than two weeks' notice. The job was a well-paying job, had reat perks like living overseas and traveling often, but I hated it. My soul was dying inside. I realized I wasn't living how I was supposed to be living, not physically, not emotionally, not intellectually, and not spiritually. The good news is that I knew where God was calling me – He wanted me to be a teacher. So, I quit my job and immediately started into graduate school to earn my master's in teaching degree. I haven't regretted that decision. This was courage. Be Not Afraid. Christ and I are an overwhelming majority.

Step 1 – check.

Step 2. Graduate student = Student Loans. Oh boy. I need some money! I found out from a friend about a Graduate Assistant position where I could work part time for education professors and make back most of my tuition cost. This was great! I applied. Thankfully, I got the last open position and began working. This was a dream come true.

Step 2– check.

Step 3. As luck, God, or fate would have it, I end up working with a professor who can only be characterized as just that – a character. We'll call him Dr. D. I sat down on Day 1 of my first semester in graduate school in Dr. D's office. He had asked me to arrive at 1pm, I arrived at 12:58 by my watch, but 1:02 by his office clock. I was late, apparently, and he appreciates punctuality. He told me that his last assistant quit halfway through the year, and he was hoping I could make it longer than that. He then proceeded to tell me that he was gay, he had multiple partners whom I may meet when they come into the office, and that if that bothered me, then I should literally get the hell out now. He then said that Christians need to keep their noses out of everybody's business and realize that their religion isn't the only religion. Oh, and that if The Supreme Court ruled to make abortion illegal, he would downright move out of the country. Oh boy! "What have I gotten myself into?" I thought. If there was anything else you could say to insult a Catholic, he said it over the next few minutes. I stopped remembering after the first few comments. Dreams – crushed. But I am not afraid.

Step 3 – eehhh, maybe a half check.

I was able to work my schedule during the fall so that I could make it to Daily Mass at noon most days. My schedule mostly consisted of working for other professors in the morning, then Mass, then working for Dr. D before going to class in the evening. The days were full and hectic, but I knew that if I was going to make it through the semester, let alone the year, I was going to have to come up with a plan (more like, ask God what his plan was). So, I did just that.

I also asked my Cursillo friends to pray for me and to pray for Dr. D, and then I resolved that, just like my mother had taught me when I was younger, if I didn't have anything nice to say, I wouldn't say anything at all. And that's what happened. Many days Dr. D would have something negative to say, but I resolved to do my job to the best of my ability no matter what. Anything he asked of me, I would do, and I would do it well. One day he asked me to empty a case of soda into his fridge, where I found a stack of mini liquor bottles. One day he asked me to clean his office, where I found a dirty change of clothes shoved into a corner. Neatly folding them, I put them on his chair. One day He asked me to replace his parking permit sticker on his motorcycle. Another day he asked me to call his sister in Seattle to see if he could stay there while he was on vacation. Once he even asked me to scratch his back because he had recently broken his arm in a motorcycle accident and was unable to reach it. Oh yeah. This is God asking me how willing I am to follow His plan. I am not afraid.

Step 4 "scratch my back and smile" – double-check

Then something started changing. He started opening up a little to me about his past life – mostly in search of pity, I imagine. I learned that he'd had cancer and beaten it and that his mother had died last April. I also heard of his many breakups with his many boyfriends and a few of his raunchy escapades under the influence of some not-quite-so-legal things. But do you know what? Something else changed, too. I started hearing a few compliments hidden amongst all the demands and orders. Things like, "You type so fast, why don't you do this for me instead?" and "You're good at organizing. Take these twenty pounds of files and folders and tell me what you think I should keep."

And then, one day, unexpectedly, Dr. D noticed my necklace. The very one I still wear today. It's a crucifix. A simple, silver crucifix given to me by a great friend of mine. I never take it off because it's the best reminder of sacrificial love. Dr. D managed to notice the necklace and he said, "Oh my. That's so beautiful. Looks very nice on you." And then a few seconds later, "Where are you with those files? Almost done?" Then it happened again a few weeks later. He noticed my necklace, as if he didn't remember complimenting me on it the first time. And again, he said, "That necklace is really beautiful." Hmm, I thought. My Cursillo brain started kicking into gear. God has a plan. I am not afraid.

Then one day I'm sorting the items in his top desk drawer, and I see it. It's a prayer card, clearly from a funeral. Mary is on the front in all her radiant glory. And I think to myself, "Huh? Why would a man like Dr. D, who swears off Christianity and any idea of Truth with a capital T, have a prayer card in his desk unless it was someone important to him?" And I remember. His mother. I resolve at once to keep following God's plan. The prayer card was my sign. "Well done, good and faithful servant. Keep going." So that's what I did. Now I'm really not afraid. Courage. Heart. Plan. Christ.

Check. Check. Check. Check. Check. Check. Check. Check.

By now it's December, the end of the semester is approaching. I'd like to say that I enjoyed working for Dr. D by then, but that wouldn't be honest. I tried my best to love him, but I mostly ended up tolerating him. Either way, I can honestly say that I tried each day to love him more. I decided I should get Dr. D something for Christmas. I'm sitting in Mass and it hits me. A crucifix. A necklace just like mine. Oh boy – should I be so bold? I can't handle this! But I remember that I don't have to. Christ and I are an overwhelming majority. My job is to say yes and do the work. Christ is in charge of the results. Ok, I told God. I'll do it.

I did. I went to the downtown Pauline bookstore and found a silver crucifix as similar to mine as I could. But I couldn't just give him a box with a necklace in it. I needed words. Good words. Solid, loving, Christ-like words. Words I can't conjure up on my own because I'm human, and all I can think about is how much this guy is everything wrong with society. Be not afraid. I prayed. I wrote the Christmas card. Here's what it I wrote:

Dr. D!! Merry Christmas! I hope this holiday season is treating you well. This is just a small gift that I hope you will appreciate. It strikes me, by the prayer card in your desk drawer, that someone close to you is Catholic. Maybe even your mom, I'm not sure. We don't t talk about faith much, but I wanted you to know that you are always welcome at church. Pope Francis has called for a year of mercy, and it has just begun. This is a year of forgiveness and love and hope. And this Christmas seemed like an appropriate time to thank you for all the guidance you've given me this past semester, but also to remind you of the "reason for the season." I hope, in this upcoming year, you can find peace, mercy, and joy. Merry Christmas, Dr. D. Love, Sarah

I gave him the gift one afternoon, and he hastily put it in his bag and said he'd open it later. No biggie. Back to work I go. But then, a few days into Christmas break, on December 18th, I get a text from him saying, "I was a bad boy and opened my present too early. You are so kind and generous! God knows I did not deserve something so wonderful! Many, many thanks."

Wow. Day MADE! I nearly jumped for joy when I got that text. But, because the Lord is never outdone in generosity, He did something even greater. Spring semester starts and I am again assigned to Dr. D. Looks like I made it longer than the last girl! A few days into working again, on January 13th, while handing me a bunch of files and folders and telling me a LOOOOONG list of things to do, Dr. D says, "Oh look! I wanna show you something!" From under his shirt he pulls out the crucifix necklace I gave him!!! He says he loves it very much and never takes it off. That it was a beautiful gift and truly undeserved. WHAT!? What is this madness?

Did I do this? Did I make this happen? No, not at all. Christ made it happen. With the capital H.I.M. all things are possible. So, what's the point of all this? The point is this – we are called by God to effect change. We're called to have courage, heart, dreams, and plans. We are all called to be Christ to those we meet.

Do not be afraid. God uniquely placed me with Dr. D this year. I was able to understand and love him in a way that no one else in his life could. I am probably the only young female Catholic he's ever encountered who would dare give him a crucifix necklace for Christmas. But do you know what? I am not afraid. Christ and I are an overwhelming majority.

MY REFLECTION ___________________________________

____

____

Speak the Truth
Christine Schwartz

I was raised in a devout Catholic home. I completed 12 years of Parochial school before enrolling in the Bachelor of Science Nursing Program at The Catholic University of America. During my student experience in Obstetrics, I had the privilege of baptizing two tiny human embryos, still in early embryonic stages. Opening the amniotic sac, I gently poured holy water on the embryos while reciting aloud the words of baptism. I also baptized a full-term infant who was born with multiple cardiac defects and died shortly after baptism. As a young, graduate nurse, while working in a secular hospital, I baptized an unknown, stillborn infant abandoned in the utility room, who would eventually end up in the laboratory.

I remembered these incidents throughout my life and, as the abortion issue became a common topic and rampant in our country, I continued to pray and speak of the value of human life from the moment of conception.

Several years ago, while cleaning out a drawer filled with old cards, letters, and photos, I found a forgotten letter written to my husband, Hal, and me by a former co-worker of Hal's. He was a professor, a Catholic, who had left the university a few years prior to my husband's departure from that same institution. We had not had contact with him since that time. Following is an excerpt from that letter:

."I saw your request for prayer for Hal in the S.C. Cursillo email line. Chris…Chris, over the years I have become Pro-Life. I remember some things you told me years ago when I was carrying on about Pro-Choice. I always date the beginning of the change in me to that conversation…"

Do I remember that situation or what I said? No. However, I undoubtedly shared my experiences as a young nurse with him and others, emphasizing my strong belief that life begins at conception. Christ taught us the importance of human dignity, just as we saw in Mary's acceptance of the Word Incarnate.

We may never know when, or if, our words or actions will have a positive influence on someone, but we do or say them anyway because we believe and have faith in how Christ taught us to live through His own words and actions. De Colores.

MY REFLECTION ___________________________________

____

____

Covid Adventure
Debbie Allen

I have a personal story to share—it is what I call my "covid adventure," as God really put me to work while others were in seclusion during the covid pandemic.

In March of 2020, my husband and I decided to buy a vacation home in Murrells Inlet, SC. We were both working a lot—he had a great job at a hospital in Columbia, and I had a thriving real estate business in Columbia. Our thought was that we needed to find a way to make some "down time." Having a place to escape to walk the beach and relax sounded ideal!

A friend (I'll call her Julie) and I went to inspect this vacation home. On our drive there Julie shared that she and her husband had been married for over 20 years, but they no longer had the same interests and were staying together for the sake of the kids. They had plans to divorce after all the children were out of the house. That made me sad. I prayed during our trip and asked God to show me how to counsel my friend. I wanted to encourage her without "butting in." I was afraid, but then I remembered: **"Christ and I are an overwhelming majority!"** After arriving at the condo and finishing the inspections, I silently prayed for God to guide me.

I received a text on my phone. It was from my husband. The text read: "I believe the Lord is speaking to me." I looked at Julie and showed her the text. She looked at me in amazement and said, "Your husband would send you a text like that?" I chuckled and said that yes, he and I have learned over **many** years that God has a plan, and our lives are so much better when we listen to HIM and follow that plan. So, I called my husband and he said, "You're not going to believe this. The department director at the hospital in Georgetown called and wants to interview me." My first thought was, "Oh no! What about my work in Columbia? Mike has a great job in Columbia, too. He can't be working at the coast while I'm in Columbia!"

And then I heard God's voice saying, "Trust ME."

So, there I was. Sitting in the car knowing that my husband was listening to God, and I was afraid of the details. And here was my friend, sitting beside me in the car, with worries about her own marriage. I prayed, and I listened, and I sensed God's nearness: "Be not afraid." I knew that God had a plan, and I needed to listen.

On our car ride back to Columbia, Julie and I talked about Mike's opportunity and discussed different ways that this could work. We talked about Mike's text and his being open to God speaking to him. I think Julie was surprised that Mike and I even discussed God's plan for our lives. I could tell that God was answering my prayer about counseling my friend. Even though we didn't talk about her marriage, Mike and I were setting an example without saying a word about her situation.

When I arrived home in Columbia, I was full of mixed emotions. Mike and I were excited about his new opportunity. But how could we live two and a half hours away from each other? How could I keep up the Columbia home on two acres while he worked in Georgetown? How could I leave my real estate business in Columbia? So many questions.

We started praying the rosary as a couple each evening and asked God for direction. For a couple of months, we enjoyed the vacation condo and discerned the path that God was leading us on. Mike was officially offered the position in May and, after much prayer, we knew that was God's plan. In the meantime, I shared the many signs that God was giving us with my friend Julie. Just by not being afraid to share how God was working in our life, Julie seemed to be more positive, more interested in our faith.

Mike started his job in Georgetown in June. I was still working in Columbia and asking God to show me how I could transition to work at the beach while maintaining my Columbia business. One afternoon, I received a phone call from the owner of my company asking me to meet him for lunch. During our meeting, he shared that he had been considering plans to expand to the Georgetown/Horry County area and my being there was perfect timing for his business plan. He didn't want me to give up my Columbia business, and I could work in both areas. Wow! Really God? This is better than any plan I could have imagined!

I shared this new opportunity with Julie. She said that she knew that this was the hand of God. Wow again! Julie was changing her attitude about life. I didn't even have to say anything about her situation. I just followed God's plan and set the example.

By now it was mid-summer. Julie's youngest child was in public high school and struggling with virtual learning. I had shared that our grandchildren had switched to Catholic school this year, and it was the best decision for them. Not long after our discussion, Julie enrolled her child in Catholic school, too. She and her husband got involved in the school and, by the end of the first semester, they knew that their decision was the best for their family. All I did was set the example by sharing our family's positive experience.

It has been over a year since that first ride with Julie to the beach condo. God has opened so many opportunities for Mike and me. We sold our home in Blythewood, built a home at the beach, and sold that condo that we bought just over a year ago. I am able to work in both areas—and when I work in Columbia, I have the privilege of living at our daughter and son-in-law's, so I get to spend lots of time with our grandchildren. Our "covid journey" was full of surprises and blessings from God.

Julie and I had lunch recently and she talked about her home situation. She told me that she is a different person than she was back then. She and her husband are doing things together and finding that they have more in common than they thought. My heart was glad, and I pray daily that their marriage will be saved, and their family will be stronger.

Did I really make a difference in Julie's life? I don't believe it was me. It was God guiding me to be a Christian example. A Christian LEADER. In the book of Philippians, it says, "I can do all things through Christ who strengthens me."

And—what started out as a dream for Mike and me to have a vacation spot turned out to be God's gift of change for us. We listened for God's voice and stepped out in faith. Our jobs changed. God gave us even better work situations. Our home changed. God gave us a home that is perfect for this time in our lives. Julie's life changed. I believe this happened because God worked through Mike and me to LEAD by CHRISTIAN example. We followed His will and good things happened. They ALWAYS do!

MY REFLECTION ____

____

____

My 4th Day – A New Life for Me
Bill Desciak

My 4th Day started, appropriately enough, by going to Group Reunion. I had been there a few times before I attended my weekend, but this time was different. For starters, I arrived early, something I rarely did in the past. As a matter of fact, I was the first person there. When Jamiel Khadri (the guy who started this Group Reunion) showedup, he immediately started to laugh when he saw me. "Wow! I can already tell you are on fire just by how you look!" I started to laugh as well.

While I didn't realize I had a different "look," I agreed with him that I felt different. More than that, I had changed.

The day before my encounter with Jamiel, I was sitting by myself on a public dock in my neighborhood. Now that I think of it, I guess THAT was when my 4th day truly began, me alone with my thoughts. And with the Holy Spirit. I recall clearly just sitting on that dock, something I had rarely made time to do in the past. I just sat and contemplated the weekend experience. What had happened? Why did I feel this way? Was this how it was always going to be moving forward? I quickly realized that, like the mystery of the Eucharist, this experience wasn't important (or even possible) to understand. It was important to just accept, through faith.

And that is what I did. Something happened, I was different, and things were going to change.

The first thing that changed was my relationship with my family. It had always been pretty solid, but now it was even better. I was more patient, more open to listening, more understanding, and frankly more fun to be around! When you allow the Holy Spirit to come in, good things happen. Not sometimes, but ALL the time.

The second thing that happened was "expansion through action." During one of our group sessions, Jamiel was telling a story about a Cursillista who used to be in our group, but who had started his own new Group Reunion with some other guys. Jamiel said, "Yeah, we miss having him here, but that's what is supposed to happen. You start talking about Cursillo, more people start going to the weekend, then you expand by having more groups. It's really a good thing that he has moved on because it is one of the ways the movement grows." That story hit home with me.

I am a parishioner at St. Benedict in Mt. Pleasant. Most of the guys in Jamiel's Group Reunion are from Christ Our King and Stella

Maris, about 30 minutes away. I started thinking about the presence of Cursillo in my home parish. What could I do to help? One morning, while sitting in my kitchen, a thought hit me. What if I said a few words about what Cursillo is, and what it has meant to me, at the end of Mass? I was immediately excited about the idea, but paused and thought, "Ok Bill, is this your ADD setting in? Another crazy idea that will lead to nowhere because of your wandering mind?" It was a legitimate question, as I have had many ideas in the past that ended up being dead ends. Maybe this was another one of those? I mean, who am I to stand up in front of our congregation and share my story? Who do I think I am, "Mr. Holy?" What would my friends think? What would EVERYONE think? And would Father Mark (our Pastor) even go for it?"

Thankfully, The Holy Spirit won out over my doubts and apprehension. As Mother Theresa once said, ***"We are not called to be successful, but faithful."*** I think being faithful means being open to the Holy Spirit with humility and with fearlessness. In short, just try.

And that's what I did. I tried.

I can go through the details another time, but in the spirit of brevity, I will close by saying that Father Mark (Good) was open and accommodating to me presenting a brief ambo talk after all the Masses at St. Benedict. This led to several men and women at St. Benedict giving Cursillo a try, which led to two new Group Reunions starting at St. Benedict, and we are still growing! While I miss my original group, Jamiel was right when he said, "This is how it is supposed to be."

In closing, I think it is important to point out that this is NOT about me at all, but about allowing the Holy Spirit to GET TO WORK! Grace is a gift that we ALL have, the good and the bad, the apathetic and the people of action. The difference between action and inaction with regards to the Holy Spirit is your willingness to "till the soil of your heart." This allows the seeds of Grace to sink in and take root...

and to grow.

It starts with prayer and humility, and usually ends with good things. But even if we fail, we should recall Mother Theresa's wise and comforting words: ***"We are not called to be successful, but faithful."*** De Colores!

MY REFLECTION ____________________________________

____

____

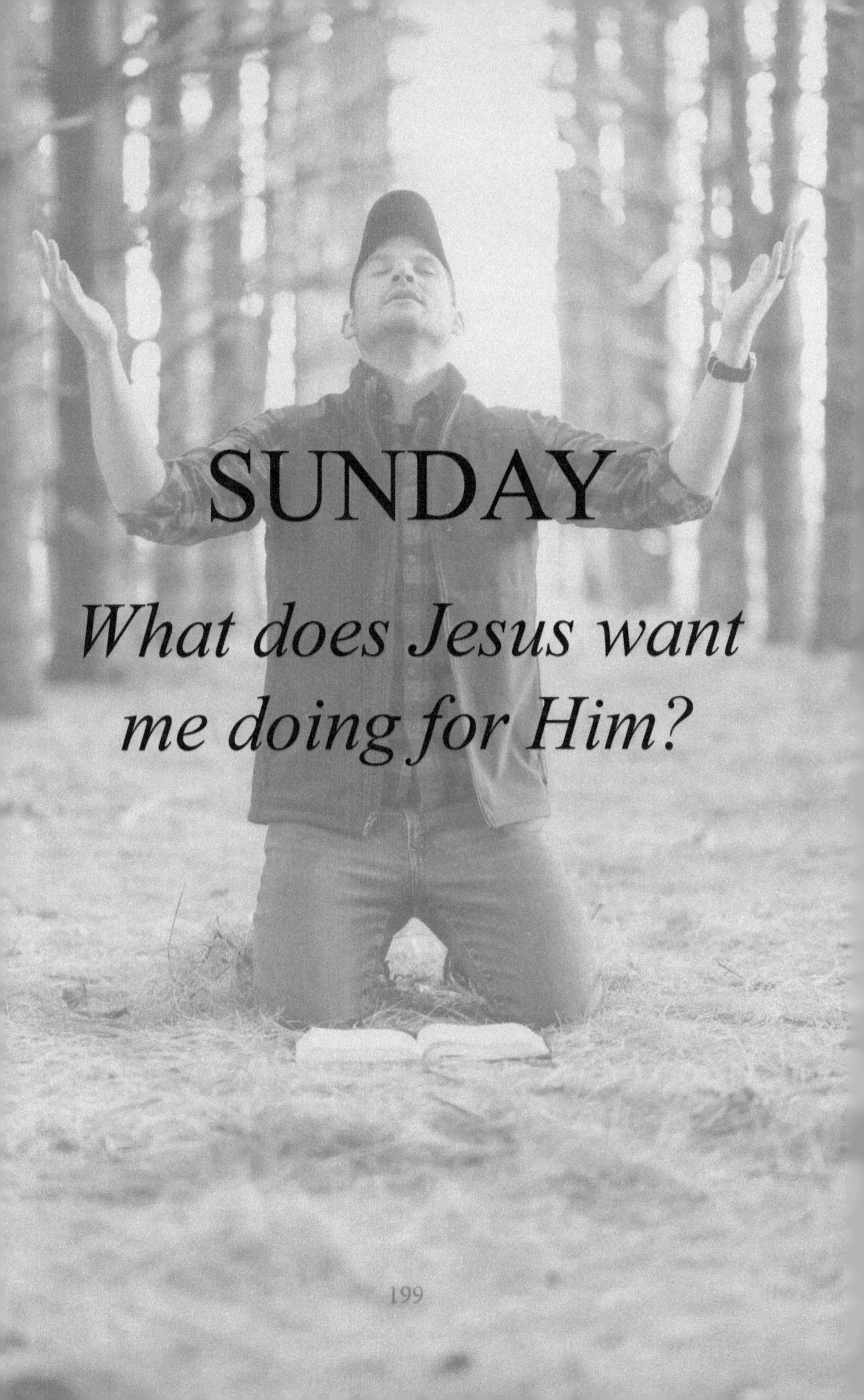

SUNDAY

What does Jesus want me doing for Him?

Chapter Fifteen

*Christ's Message to
the Cursillistas*

Christ's Message to the Cursillistas Summary
Deacon Robert Pierce

Something amazing happens every Cursillo weekend. The people who arrive on Thursday are not the same as those who return home on Sunday. One way to understand the Cursillo is to see that it is like the time Jesus spent forming His Apostles. Entering the final phase of the Cursillo weekend, it helps to reflect on Jesus's final words to the Twelve. It is a verse that I want to split into two parts. The first part is: You did not choose me; no, I chose you… (John 15:16)

That is a scary thought – Jesus chose YOU -- but you know in your heart that it is true. I know I was scared on the retreat before my ordination. Not because of the difficulty of tasks that I would be asked to do, but because I was making a permanent, public commitment, to be a lifelong servant of God and His people. It is an imposing thought. While you may not have been ordained to the same type of service as I have, your commitment is no less permanent or public. You've been baptized; you have publicly received Confirmation. You hear the same words at the end of Mass that I do: "Go forth! The Mass is ended." It is not "please go." It is a command, "Go."

It should not surprise you that I draw comfort from St. Therese of Lisieux who said, "This is the mystery of my vocation, my whole life, and of the special graces given me by Jesus. He does not call those who are worthy, but those He chooses."

Jesus brought us to a Cursillo weekend for a purpose. We encounter Him in new ways. We encounter Him like the disciples on the road to Emmaus. Our hearts burn as we hear the message of the scriptures, maybe really for the first time. We meet Him in the breaking of bread. Like the apostles at the Transfiguration, we have seen the glory of the Lord revealed in new ways in ourselves and each other. And like the Apostles at the Transfiguration, we would like to stay on this mountaintop forever. But, as with the apostles, this mountain vision is given in order to prepare us for valley duty: … and I commissioned you to go forth and to bear fruit, fruit that will last. (John 15:16)

We are called apart. We are called to be different. Jesus brings us to Cursillo to send us to do His work in the world. The call of the Cursillo does not end with our own lives—it must be lived in our environments. We are to bear the fruit of evangelization. This is the fruit that will endure.

Jesus had only a few followers after three years of ministry. We imagine that the Son of God ought to have been more successful. What we fail to understand is the strategy Jesus is teaching us for reaching our world—that of building Christian community.

I guess you can say Jesus was conducting Cursillo #1 in the Diocese of Galilee. He taught them to pray (Piety/Holiness), he instructed and formed them (Study/Formation), and he sent them into action to evangelize and proclaim the Good News. Most important, He spent His time forming the Twelve as a community, meals and discussions around a fire, knowing that His work would endure as long as they remained united.

The world sees our unity – the unity of believers is a witness even more powerful and profound than any single person could provide. One person could be an anomaly, but a group is the sign of something that is attractive, something that gives a sense of hope. Those who have the courage to witness in front of abortion clinics relate how they are often approached by people who don't necessarily agree with them, but nonetheless thank them because they gave that corner of utter darkness a sense of hope.

It is only as a genuine Christian community that we are a sign of His presence to the world. We cannot be effective in the apostolate alone. We must be united to the Body of Christ, that is, each other. While remaining united to each other, we must similarly remain united to the Head. Our effectiveness, as individual Christians and as a community, also depends on our living union with Jesus: "Whoever remains in me, with me in him, bears fruit in plenty; for cut off from me you can do nothing." (John 15:5)

In Jesus, we have a revolutionary power: "I tell you most solemnly, whoever believes in me will perform the same works as I do myself; He will perform even greater works." (John 14:12) But the works – or the great work – start with who you become. The power to transform society emanates because **you** become an instrument of the Holy Spirit. Cursillo is not about joining organizations; rather Cursillo is about being Jesus to others. And the truth is that you are not going to be able to change environments just by joining them, but by being different men and women – different because you live in faith knowing that "Christ and I are an overwhelming majority."

Nonetheless, it does not matter whether we are doing the seemingly impossible or the very ordinary. By His life, Jesus sanctified all human activity. The mark of a true disciple is that in whatever they do, in whatever environments God has placed them, they bear fruit, calling others to discipleship, for the glory of God. The challenge should not frighten us. All we have to do is to bear witness to what we know to be true about Jesus's victory. "Have courage, I have overcome the world!" (John 16:33)

The weekend goes by like a flash, but hopefully, we truly recognize that the encounter between Jesus and Peter at the end of the Gospel is for all who accept responsibility for the Gospel. Do you love me? Feed my lambs. Tend my sheep. Be my hands and feet and face to a people who dwell in darkness. Come, follow me.

An Introvert's Guide to Evangelization –
The Cursillo Approach
Vincent Weaver

About 25 years ago, I started to discover the faith of my childhood. I read dozens and dozens of books on apologetics, Church history, and Church teaching on a wide variety of challenging subjects. Naturally, I assumed that I was now ready to go out and change the hearts and minds of everyone to whom I relayed this wonderful information! Funny thing, though – evangelization doesn't work that way. Who knew? Turns out, most of the Christians of the early Church knew this, and yet they were wildly successful with leading others to Christ, even amid the most brutal of circumstances.

I recently attended a weekend retreat where Church historian Mike Aquilina gave a series of talks. All the talks were fantastic, but one of those centered on friendship – the vehicle through which most conversions took place during those first three centuries, and still take place today. During the course of that presentation, Mr. Aquilina referenced the work of sociologist Rodney Starks (particularly in *The Rise of Christianity*), who used a rational, data-driven means of calculating the growth pattern of Christianity up through the year 350 AD. Incredibly, the ranks of Christians grew by *40% per decade* for those first 300 years! (*And contrary to popular belief, the rate likely did NOT spike after Emperor Constantine gave his official endorsement, but rather continued for the next several decades before leveling off a bit in the mid-fourth century.*)

While that rate of growth would seem to be only attributable to miracles or mass conversions, the explanation is probably much more mundane – and compelling. The work of Rodney Starks (and others he cites) shows that throughout history, people convert to a belief system when there is a meaningful relationship with someone who is already an adherent to those beliefs. While some may feel called to stand on street corners and preach the Gospel, or to knock on doors of strangers to tell them about Jesus, conversions rarely happen like this. Instead, those early Christians made friends with others – regardless of social class – and then those friendships made their friends Christians. Strong family relationships had a similar effect. This same principle holds true today. This is how Mormonism spreads – through <u>networks of family and friends</u>. All those missionaries riding their bikes knocking on doors of strangers lead to a conversion rate of only about 1 per 1000. However, when a family member or close friend is also a Mormon, the rate approaches 50%. The same dynamic holds true for others from Moonies to Scientologists to Wiccans, and as different as these ideologies are from Catholicism, there's a wonderful lesson here that we can all make use of – meaningful friendships bring others to Christ.

So, as we lament the recent spike in <u>people claiming to be "nones"</u> or atheists or agnostics, it makes sense that as most turn more to technology and superficial "friends" on social media, the impact we have as Christians plummets (<u>along with our mental health</u>). If you are like me, though, an introvert – the temptation is to embrace this social isolation. It is more comfortable, after all! But I'm realizing lately that this isn't what we're called to do – we are all called to preach the Gospel. While that may sound like a daunting task, the truth is that it's all about investing time – face-to-face time – in developing deep, meaningful friendships and relationships with our family members. Not only are we doing ourselves a favor when we spend our time on such endeavors, but we give others a chance to see and experience the reason for our joy.

And this is where Cursillo comes in. This is precisely their mantra: "Make a friend. Be a friend. Bring a friend to Christ." Why didn't I see this obvious connection before?!? You don't need precise and brilliant explanations of the Catechism. You don't need earth-shattering charisma. All you need is to show others they matter to you. And you do that by making time for them on a regular basis and loving them. Whether you're an introvert or an extrovert, commit to regular time building those friendships (*but don't forget your family!*) Ask them to tell their story. Ask them what interests them and why. Ask them what's important to them. Then listen and just be a friend. The focus doesn't have to be on a huge number of people. Just a handful will create a ripple effect beyond what we can imagine. So, let's take a tip from those early Christians. Rediscover friendship. If enough of us make a habit of this, we just may see that elusive, re-Christianization of the world take place after all!

MY REFLECTION ____

____

____

A Guide for the Cowardly Evangelist
Sharon Shymansky Roberts

I am not a very brave Evangelist. I am great around my Catholic friends but, put me out into the real world away from the security of my parish community, and I am uncomfortable. However, I have come to believe that this discomfort is exactly where God wants us to be when we are doing His work. When we are uncomfortable, we are more likely to turn to Him for the words we need. (Luke 12:11-12 "Don't worry how you will respond, and don't worry what you should say. The Holy Spirit will give you the words to say at the moment you need them." I try to remember that scripture when I am in a situation where I can obviously do or say one small thing to bring God into the situation. But make no mistake, I also take a deep breath and send a quick prayer to heaven!

Here are five very quick evangelistic things I have tried, with success, I might add. Think about them. Try them. If you are like me, you will leave the situation thanking Him for the chance to bring someone just a millisecond closer to Him. Hmmm. How many milliseconds would that be if every Christian in the world did something similar just once a day? (No clue. I taught English to middle, high school, and college students! I avoided math like the plague!)

1. I bought a dozen copies of Matthew Kelly's *Holy Moments*. I put one in my purse and stacked the others on the back seat of my car. Each time I go through a drive-in food establishment, if the cashier is smiling and pleasant, I usually say something like, "Thank you for smiling and being so pleasant. I'd like to give you this book. I think, after you read it, you will find many more moments to smile about in your day. God loves you. Have a blessed day!" I then hand the cashier a book and drive to the next window. See what a coward I am? Do I know what they do with the books? Not usually. I do remember one time when I revisited a McDonald's and recognized the cashier who had been a recipient of a book. I said, "You probably don't remember me, but I gave you a small book a few weeks ago, *Holy Moments*. I wonder, did you like it?"

"Oh my gosh," she exclaimed. "I did! I read it and I passed it on to my girlfriend to read. I really liked it. Thank you again!" That was nice to hear. Spreading the Word!

2 . Let's stick with the drive-thru scenario. About three years ago, at my neighborhood McDonald's during the entire month of December, I began paying for the food order for the car behind me. (I must confess I love McDonald's Caramel mocha coffee and used to go at least three times weekly to this establishment for my coffee fix.) As I pulled up to the cashier (her name is Tommy), I would tell her to also give me the ticket for the car behind me. The first couple of times, she was a bit flustered and didn't understand what I wanted to do. We eventually overcame that. Anyway, she would give me both receipts, I would pay them, and then I would carefully instruct her, "Tommy, please tell them I said to have a blessed day. Can you do that for me?" She would agree, and I would pull away to the next window to pick up my order. Some people would honk their horns in a thank you. Most would do nothing. Either response was ok. I just prayed they would remember the time someone paid for them and would, one day, pay it forward as well. One time, I had to pull beyond the second window to wait for my order. The woman in the car behind me apparently got her order, and as she pulled alongside me, she lowered her driver's window. I looked her way. She was crying! "I just wanted to thank you so much for what you just did. I have already had a terrible morning. My son is sick, and I have to get him and take him to the doctor. I'm going to be late for work. And then I found out you paid for our breakfast and wished me a blessed day. My day just got a whole lot brighter because of you. I just wanted to thank you!" She smiled, waved, and drove away. Wow! Thank you, Jesus, for *that* holy moment.

Now I don't wait until December. Whenever the mood strikes me, I pay for the car behind me. Full confession: my husband Dan has learned from a barista how to make McDonald's caramel mocha at home, so I rarely go there anymore. But when I do, I pay for two. Every

December, I still make a concentrated effort to make at least a weekly visit and pay for the car behind me. It just seems like the right thing to do during Christmas! Oh, a word of caution…McDonald's has started the McDonald's app, and many people pay when they order on the app. Quite a few times I have been disappointed because I couldn't pay for the car behind me; they had already paid on the app. I think I need to find a new drive-thru…

3. This next idea I stole from a friend. He always has a line of scripture or a famous Christian quote in his signature line on his emails. He is, through that one line, letting his email recipients know how he feels about his faith. Now I do that too. My current quote is from Venerable Archbishop Fulton J Sheen. *The greatest love story of all time is contained in a tiny white host.* No one has said anything about it, but I feel good proclaiming my faith in that way. Who knows? Maybe others will start doing that, too.

4. The simplest of all is to choose a ringtone for your phone that reflects your favorite religious song. My ringtone is "Hallelujah." I chose a version by a Southern Maryland band, because Southern Maryland is the home of my heart. (Full disclosure: I now live in Pawleys Island, SC, and this is the home of my soul!) Anyway, when people hear my ringtone, they know I am a Christian! Many have commented on it and we begin talking about how much we love the song and end up talking about God! So easy!

5. Buy and wear Christian-based tee shirts! Of, course, my favorite place is www.thechosengifts.com, but there are many other sites out there. One of my favorite tees says, "Come and See." People would ask what it meant. (That told me they never watched The Chosen tv series.) I would tell them about The Chosen and we would be talking "Jesus" in no time! My favorite story though, is when I would wear it as a greeter to Mass. As a church greeter, my job is to welcome everyone to Mass and to open the door for them. Each time I would wear the shirt, people would say, "Come and see what?" and I would answer, "Jesus."

These are such simple things. They take little money or time but go a long way in helping me to feel like I am, albeit in small ways, fulfilling my Cursillo mission of helping to bring the world to Christ. Doing His work by spreading His love, even in small ways, makes me happy and I hope it makes Him smile.

MY REFLECTION _______________________________

____

____

The Holy Spirit at Work!
Diane Bayless

It all started some time ago with *The Chosen* and Matthew Kelly's *Holy Moments*. When Matthew threw out the challenge of helping to spread a billion copies of HM, I accepted the challenge. However, how do I do that in a neighborhood where few people go to church? I couldn't do it at the daily happy hour as politics and religion are taboo!

I started with folks to whom I had given devotionals from *The Chosen*. My surgeon is Catholic, and I had given him several books over the two years he has worked on replacing my knees. On one occasion I asked if he had been reading them.

"My life is going a million miles every day and then I have a 5-minute break. One of the books you gave me is just perfect. I can't remember the name, but the readings are short to read and think on as I go about my day."

"*Holy Moments*?"

"Yes, *Holy Moments* and I've shared my thoughts with colleagues." "Would you like more copies?"

"Absolutely", and I gave him four of them!

Another time, during a neighborhood get-together, one of the women came up to me and asked to speak privately. "We need to pray for our country, do a Bible study or something and will you lead it?" Ironically, or maybe the Holy Spirit was working, Dr. Allen Hunt's new Bible study on Genesis had arrived that day. I told her I would give her several books to browse through and let me know. The next day her text was all about *Holy Moments*. "I wish I had had a book like this when I was in high school. Maybe I wouldn't have made so many mistakes. How can I get more for my children and nieces?" I gave her eight! Our first book club session will be on August 4, 2023, when more people are back from vacations.

I have left copies of HM in the back of the church, given some to my PT person when she came to the house after my knee surgery, and have taken several to rehab. I knew Rick, who works at the rehab, was Christian as he had a devotional on his desk shelf. He took several, one for himself and the others in the waiting room. The next time I came in he told me that people were reading them!

Another time I went to my cardiologist and asked the woman at the desk if I might leave a few books in the waiting area. "What is it?" one of the gals asked who was checking me in. "It's about working with God. Are you a Christian?"

"Yes!"

"Would you like one?"

"Yes!"

"And so would I," said another gal behind the desk. All four of them took one!

My girlfriend from Michigan came to visit. She is another prayer warrior, a non-practicing Catholic who was once a Eucharistic

Minister. I pray for her daily and hope the Spirit works in her heart as she took 16 copies of HM home to her Bible group. She recently called to tell me about a holy moment she had with her family during a reunion. She has often said, "…if anyone will bring me back to the church, it will be you!"

The strangest encounter happened early one morning. I love to walk to the beach in our neighborhood, saying my rosary while walking to the sunrise. This particular morning, there was a strange car parked at the entrance, and I saw the silhouette of a man fishing from the beach. I hesitated as the thought, "If I'm to die today, I'm ready!" ran through my head. As I approached him he turned, and we both said, "Good morning."

I walked past him about ten feet, stopped, and after a minute or so I said, "I usually walk over here for my morning prayers and to watch the sunrise. Would you mind if I stay?"

"No, no. Go right ahead!"

I went about six feet further, found my chair hidden in the bushes, pulled it out, returned to a sandy area, and settled in to listen to my phone via Bluetooth. It may have been The God Minute or Bishop Barron's daily reflection or Fr. Mike's CIY. I don't recall which. A couple of minutes later, I realized he was speaking to me. Stopping the phone and removing the ear device, I turned to him. "May I ask you a question?" he queried.

"Sure!"

"What would you tell someone who wanted to turn their life around and do good?"

Surprised by the question and his apparent sincerity, I waited a few seconds before responding. "For me, it's important to start my day with gratitude. I thank the Lord for all the blessings He showers on me, a good night's rest, waking up to a new day, family, friends, the ability to walk over here to watch the sunrise." He then proceeded to tell me about an accident, of being hit while on his motorcycle and left for dead. His leg had been broken and bent over his shoulder, and he had a large gash on his side. He shared how he remembered hearing a cop say he wouldn't make it. But he did make it, after several weeks in the hospital. He wanted to do right for his 6-year-old son, teach him the good things and get his life started on the right track. "Are you Christian?" I asked.

"Yes!"

"If I give you a book on how to work with God, will you read it?"

"Yes!" He then told me his name was Karol, and he had helped my neighbor Dalton fix the white truck that had been sitting in the yard, partially dismantled for the last two years. Being a diesel mechanic, he had gotten it back together. As Dalton lives a few houses from me and there are strange men coming and going all the time, I asked a neighbor to deliver the book to Dalton, with instructions for Dalton to give it to Karol the next time he was there. Mission accomplished!

Once, when our mail lady came to the door for a signature, I asked her if I could put a copy of HM in every mailbox. "No, as you would be stealing from the USPO, but I can put some in the Post Office foyer!"

"Would you like this one?"

"Yes, please!"

The next day I took several to the post office, and the gal behind the window was so glad to see them. I had already given her one and she wanted more.

The strangest encounter, though, was at the gas station. I had just left choir practice and, as I got out of the car, I was still humming one of the songs. A tall man on the other side of the pump said," Someone's happy today!"

"Yes, I just left our choir practice for the church service tomorrow."

"What church?"

I told him, and then asked, "Are you a Christian?"

"No…but I go to church!"

"Say what?" I thought. "Where do you go to church?" Then he proceeded to tell me about a little church north of town. About that time a woman came towards us from the station and said, "I used to be Episcopalian". I think she was his mother. I asked the man if he would like a book about working with God and he replied that he would. Mom piped up and said she wanted one, too!

Now I have a case of HM in my car, and I carry some in my purse. If I can strike up a conversation with someone, I do. Usually, seconds later I pop the question, "Are you a Christian?" If the answer is "yes" you know they will get a book. I was able to share seven of them recently by the time I got to my hubby's room as he was being discharged from the hospital.

I truly believe the world is hungry for the Lord! People are afraid of what is coming for our country. If one person reads *Holy Moments* and can collaborate with God, maybe that person will be saved and will be able to share and save others.

Thank you, Lord for working through me and allowing me to … Be Bold, Be Catholic!

MY REFLECTION ____

____

____

Chapter Sixteen

*Study of the
Environment*

Study of the Environment Summary
Tommy Smith

Sunday morning! Day 4! It has been such a grand weekend. Our expectations have been met or, in many cases, far exceeded. Time to go home. But wait. There is still a lot of work to be done to get ready to go back to the real world. Our last Rollo on Saturday opened us to the thought that we are all called to be leaders. We were told that "Christ and I are an overwhelming majority." That lays the basis of what comes next. Sunday brings us to the work that God has for us as we go out to meet the world in what Cursillo calls "Our Fourth Day". It begins with "The Study of the Environment."

We were told that the weekend was not to just make good people for Jesus but to forge leaders to go out into the world and change it for Our Lord. The definition of an environment is "the sum of ideas, persons, and circumstances that occur in a specific time and place when people get together." If we are with people, we are in an environment. And the environments need to be won over. If we do not do our part to win the environments for Christ, that environment will not stay neutral. Something or someone will win it, and we know by experience that eventually, if good Christians do nothing, it is most likely going to be the evil one who wins.

The environment consists of three separate battlefronts: ourselves, others and the combination of the two. We discovered that we need a battle plan for all three. To get ourselves ready we need to first align our will to God's purpose and then, second, we pray. Talk to God first before we talk to others about God. Third, we need to put our mind to work. We need to think about ways to approach the environment. And lastly, we need to be all in with our heart. These are the weapons with which God has armed us.

In thinking about "the others in the environment,"we learned that "others" fit into five different groups and therefore how we approach them needs to be prayerfully thought out. Group one loves God and wants to do good. Group two loves God and wants to feel good. Group three believes in God and nothing more. The fourth group does not believe in God because they do not know God. The fifth group does not believe in God because they believe He does not exist. Each of these "others" clearly has differing needs and therefore different approaches.

When we engage others, our battle plan and the order of the weapons we use changes somewhat. We first must take the risk to put our heart before our head. We must be passionate about changing the environment. People are more swayed by our passion then they are by intellectual arguments. Then we can put our minds to work. Our will can now be fueled. Lastly, we put it in Jesus' hands in prayer.

The last front is the environment and that requires commitment born out of love for Our Lord and Savior Jesus Christ. Will this be easy? Probably not. Will there be risks? Undoubtedly. Will it require our best efforts? Absolutely! Yet, we are the ones Jesus has put onto the battlefield. He obviously has great faith in us. And as we learned last night, we must, "Bloom where we are planted."

MY REFLECTION _______________________________________

____

____

The Mantra
Theresa Marie

Right before my Cursillo weekend, I accepted a new job as a practice manager for a physician's office. It was never a position I aspired to reach. I am a nurse! I love patient care, but the opportunity came at a time when I had just started searching for something different. I prayed God would make something available to me if that was His will. Less than a week later, I got a call from one of the physicians offering the position to me. After much prayer, I accepted the job and felt it was what the Lord wanted for me.

Right after my weekend, I was chatting with a coworker who knew nothing about my special Cursillo weekend. During the same weekend, however, he heard a message at church, and when he heard it, he thought of my new job and wanted to share the message with me. The message? "Bloom where you are planted." Amazing… goosebumps! I, too, heard that message over the weekend and had the same thoughts about my new position and what God had in store for me. I had felt a stirring in me during that weekend talk, as I was about to embark on a completely new path with new people. I also knew going into the job that there were some strong personalities I would encounter.

During Lent, another couple invited my husband and me to do a study with them called Fearless. It was a study to recognize fears in our lives and how to battle them and be set free from these fears. In week one, I identified my fear of failing at this new job. Over the course of the next few weeks, I experienced chaos, frustration with staff, and I felt like I had nowhere to turn. I felt like my only resort was to quit this job. No human was built to tolerate this much stress. I had relapsed back into my controlling tendencies. I thought I had surrendered those to Jesus at my Cursillo weekend, but here I was, just a few weeks later, frustrated because I couldn't gain control of my work environment! I had forgotten to trust in God. I wrote a resignation letter and gave my one month notice to the doctors at the end of the day on a Thursday. I was done! I came in to work on Friday to balloons, a card of encouragement, and a gift of random prayer cards from a dear friend to lift my spirits. I drew a card that read, "Have patience, God is not finished yet." I felt so conflicted. Did God really want me to stay and change this environment for Him, or was He telling me this particular environment was doing me more harm than good? I decided to stay a bit longer.

Later, in sharing my craziness with some dear friends, I was made aware of the spiritual enemies that are constantly around us that want to cause us to feel unsettled and chaotic. Then, I was introduced to the world of binding prayers! How amazing is God's timing as, a week after learning about and praying binding prayers, I had the blessing of hearing and seeing, in person, Father Ripperger, an exorcist, speak on the presence of demons and how to combat them. How amazing again that a few weeks later, Father Ripperger was a speaker in one of the videos from the Fearless series and spoke on using binding prayers! I don't think God could have been any timelier with revealing to me tools for the daily spiritual battle, and He made it clearly known to me that I am not alone, He is with me.

One of the first pieces of homework of the Fearless series was to come up with a mantra to help with times when fears arise. I could not think of one at first and did not have one to report back to the group when we met again. It was weeks later, after all the binding prayers, I stayed at my job, the dust settled, demons were beaten, and there was peace around me that I was reminded of my Cursillo weekend and the mantra that I had already adopted. I had relinquished control of my life to Jesus, and I now repeat to myself daily, "Jesus, I trust in you."

Do You Love Enough?
Neil Fico

Two years ago, in September, my mother passed away from a long battle with dementia. My mother was 78 years old when she passed; she had been living in my hometown of Pittsburgh with my sister and her family until being moved into an assisted living facility. She had suffered and struggled with dementia for over five years. During this time, my sister Beth, who is my only sibling, had been our mother's main support and caretaker, taking care of mom at her home for the first four years, before mom was admitted to assisted living.

My sister is married and has two children who were living at home and participating in taking care of my mom as her condition continued to deteriorate. My mother began suffering from personality changes caused by the dementia which made her very irritable at times and difficult to deal with.

My sister and her family's ability to take care of Mom at home became unmanageable, so we decided to place her in assisted living. It was a very difficult decision. My sister suffered from regret and resentment since the responsibility of taking care of Mom had fallen on her and her family. Her relationships with her husband and kids had been challenged in a way that I began recognizing by the way they treated each other, including our mother.

My sister and I spent many nights on the phone talking about Mom's condition. I could sense my sister's sadness and stress. It seemed like all that I could do to help was to listen to her and to the challenges she faced daily. It was a desperate situation. While all this was going on, I could sense my sister starting to resent my mother for being so needy and demanding of her time. I could also sense resentment towards me for not being with her and being able to help with our mother.

At certain times, when I was able, I would fly home to visit, and whenever I was there, it would bring consolation to my sister. But as soon as I left, all the pressure was placed back on her and her family. As all this was going on, I would share my feelings with my wife, Becky. I explained to Becky that my fear was the stress of all of this may permanently damage the relationships between my sister and myself or my sister and her family members.

One day, as I was sharing all this with Becky, out of the blue, she pointed out how Beth and her family were primed and ready to be re-evangelized in their Catholic faith. Then Becky asked if I had asked Beth about attending Mass or if she had talked to a priest. I stood speechless for a second. Then, with a real, intense apostolic ego, I said, "No. Beth doesn't want me talking to her about the Church. She hasn't been to a Sunday Mass in years, and she probably would say something mean, and then say something disparaging about the Catholic Church."

Becky looked at me, you know the way wives do before they humble you, and said, "You ARE her brother. You should want your mother to be in heaven!"

What Becky was seeing and I wasn't is how God sees things. I was fruitless in trying to ease my sister of the stress and difficulties she and her family were going through because I wasn't being apostolic in my actions toward my sister. I never prayed about the way I should approach my sister. I wasn't resolute, enthusiastic, or joyful because I wasn't looking at things the way God looks at things. My actions to try and help my sister, while having good intentions, were without any

Christian intention to evangelize my sister and bring her into a closer relationship with Christ. God had another plan, and he needed me to cooperate with it.

Let me share with you a little background about my relationship with my sister, Beth. My sister and I were both raised Catholic, and we grew up like many brothers and sisters do, fighting and aggravating one another. We loved each other as brother and sister, but we had very little in common other than we had the same parents. Therefore, we did not spend a lot of free time together. Our father passed away while we were both still in high school, and Beth quickly drifted away from her Catholic upbringing. She graduated high school and met some people who introduced her to some new-age religion, and she soon began engaging in the occult and hanging out with people who got her involved with drugs and alcohol.

She attended beauty school, became a hairstylist, got married, and had two children. They were both raised Catholic. One is my goddaughter. My sister never attends Mass on Sundays and has a very secular view of the world, so we often don't see eye to eye on things. This makes it very difficult to talk to her at times. So, until my mother became ill, we would rarely go out of our way to pick up the phone and call one another.

Thus, Becky, being as observant as she is, pointed out how little time Beth and I had spent in contact with one another. During those infrequent talks, Becky continued, the topic of my mother's funeral and funeral arrangements had never been brought up. She questioned when, if ever, I was going to ask my sister if she had planned for a Catholic funeral for my mother. Becky knew it was extremely important to me to have a Catholic burial for Mom and for her to receive her last rites. The problem was that I wasn't sure if my mother had planned in her will for a Catholic burial. If Mom had not put that request in her will, what would Beth do if I insisted on it? I also had doubts that Beth would arrange these proceedings on her own. These concerns made me very uneasy.

Why was it so difficult for me to discuss such important things with my sister? It's our Catholic faith and the salvation of our mother's soul. Was it due to the fear of offending my sister? My mother's Catholic burial arrangements and her being given last rites are obviously more important than offending my sister, right?

Finally, I took it to prayer. What God revealed to me was the real reason I was hesitant to talk to my sister about our Catholic faith. It wasn't because of fear of offending my sister. It was due to a lack of authentic Christian love for my sister! I didn't love my sister enough with authentic Christian love to act apostolically. I knew that I loved my Mom enough to act apostolically, but my sister? That required sacrifice!

I finally picked up the phone and called my sister. We had our first real conversation about how much we truly care for our mother. We each wanted her soul in heaven with our dad. I acted in love toward both my mother and sister by insisting that Mom have a Catholic burial and that I would do whatever was needed to make the arrangements for my mother's anointing and funeral Mass. To my shock and surprise, my sister, without me knowing, had made all the arrangements for our mother's Catholic Mass and burial. She knew how important it was to me.

In hindsight, my sister was the one who was apostolically acting more than myself for our mother. When my Mom did finally pass, she had a beautiful Catholic burial. My family and my sister's family celebrated my mother's life, knowing that we had mutually loved our mother enough to put aside any resentment toward each other that we may have had.

My sister and her family still don't go to Mass on Sundays, but I'm going to continue reaching out apostolically to them with the hope that Christ will work through me in Christian love. Jesus is calling each one of us in our own way to build up his kingdom. Pray. Be vigilant. Have faith. God will do the rest.

Answering His Call…Reluctantly
Sharon Shymansky Roberts

Several months ago, I started reading the book *What Would St Monica Do?* by Patti MaGuire Armstrong and Roxane Beauclair Salonen. Page 165 really spoke to me. On that page, a well-known radio host was describing the day she felt compelled to share the TRUTH with her expansive radio audience. She began her program by announcing that she was the mother of two children, both of whom were in heaven because of abortion. She admitted she had bought into the Planned Parenthood lies. But, she confessed, she could never unsee the group of people standing outside the facility on both occasions praying for her and her baby. She ashamedly admitted that she had loudly scoffed and even presented an offensive gesture to them. Still, she could never unsee them. It took 10 years but, eventually, she was led to the truth, Jesus Christ. She wanted all those men and women who were praying outside the clinic on those days, and those who still pray outside of abortion facilities everywhere, to know that while they had not made a difference in her babies' lives, they eventually made a huge impact on hers. She urged every one of you who has the courage to confront evil on the battleground in front of abortion clinics to keep doing it, and she wanted you to know that you do make a difference.

I reread that page several times, fully intending to photocopy it and give it to our Right to Life leader as encouragement for her and others. I never did and, until today, I never knew why. Today, as I ran late into mass, I passed our church bus parked outside the main church doors. I recalled that a group from our church would be going to Planned Parenthood today after mass to pray for all those inside the facility. At some point during mass, the Holy Spirit spoke to my heart and told me what He wanted me to do. I squirmed and cringed through the remainder of mass, until I received the Eucharist. It was then I prayed for the wisdom and courage to do His will..

He never promised His call to action would be comfortable. In fact, as his apostles found out, the call is more often uncomfortable. After mass, I walked outside to the bus where those parishioners who were going to the Planned Parenthood protest were gathering. I asked the leader if I could say something to the group before they boarded. She agreed, if I would agree to take their picture, so I did. Then I hesitantly told them the story of the well-known radio host and how she began her program one day. I shared her request that they keep doing what they were doing and that it did make a difference, and then I told them how much I admired them, and I confessed that I am unable to do what they do. I am too emotionally affected by the idea of babies being brutally murdered behind those walls to even pray effectively when I am there.

Then I left. I have no idea what they thought about me sharing. It did not matter. I had done what I was asked to do. I do know a few of the women were crying when I talked, so at least some hearts were touched. Thank you God, for giving me a different kind of courage and the ability to listen and do Your will.

Chapter Seventeen

Life in Grace

Life in Grace Summary
Deacon Coleman Parks

The secret to moving closer to God is to live a life in Grace. That life in Grace consists of the theological virtues of Faith, Hope and Charity, or acts of Love. These are the virtues that bring light to your life and deepen your capacity to grow in friendship with God and others.

Faith - Faith enables us to believe in God and believe in all that He has said and revealed to us. "Blessed are those that have not seen yet believe." This is the essence of Faith.

Hope - Hope enables us to desire eternal happiness and to trust in God and the promises of Christ.

Charity (Acts of Love) – Charity enables us to love God above all other things. The Bible tells us that God is pure love, and it also tells us that we were made in the image and likeness of our God. Being made in the LIKENESS of God means that God made us to love, just as He loves us.

To live continually in God's Grace means we must be oriented toward the will of God. When we live in Him, He then lives in us. The wisest thing that we can ever do is to do the will of God. Where do we learn what the will of God is? In the Bible. This is God speaking to us through this book written thousands of years ago. His words still ring true and those words, read and meditated upon daily, increase our belief and our faith.

Through study and reading about the Life of Christ, we can know what God wants. He wants us to love Him and love our neighbor with sacrificial love and to live upright lives. To help make this possible, He gives us the Grace of the Sacraments. With Grace enlightening our reason with the truths of the Faith, we can know what God wants in general and, therefore, be able to properly apply this wisdom to the concrete circumstances of our lives, thus living a life in Grace. With the wisdom and knowledge of Holy Scripture, we have a much better chance of staying the course to heaven by living according to the will of God.

To maintain, preserve, and strengthen our life in Grace, it is necessary to realize the value of these virtues, of practicing piety in our lives in an orderly way and daily. If to make God a central part of your life, then you must speak to Him regularly. You can find a good list of these practices of piety in your Pilgrims Guide, but the best practice of all is prayer. Prayer is the natural expression of our relationship with God. When we pray, we are literally MEETING with God, taking ourselves to Him in a deeply personal conversation. While prayer can take many forms (vocal prayer, meditation, "lectio divina", Liturgy of the Hours, contemplative…). What is important is that you make prayer time a habit.

The next opportunity you have to grow your life in Grace comes at Mass. You don't simply ATTEND Mass and just let the Priest say the prayers. You participate by saying these beautiful liturgical prayers with the priest. The Eucharistic Celebration is our most sacred liturgy. It is the source and summit of Christian life, the moment heaven and earth meet. Learn these prayers, follow them, pray them with the priest and the fullness and beauty of our faith will bring you to tears. Sing the songs! Sing loudly and with heart. Those songs are praising our Lord! RECEIVE THE EUCHARIST knowing with all your heart what you are receiving – the true presence of your Lord Jesus Christ - His Body and Blood. There is no greater gift.

To continue living your life in Grace, visit the Blessed Sacrament regularly. It is there you will be blessed beyond measure. Say the Rosary daily as our Mother asks us to do. Perform an Examination of Conscience daily in the morning or before retiring to bed. Lastly, seek the regular wisdom and counsel of a qualified spiritual director to help guide you on your journey.

By living your faith, staying hopeful, and sharing your love of God and neighbor, your life will be Grace-filled. And your friendship with God will be "Rock solid."

MY REFLECTION ____

____

____

Saying YES with Song
Debbie Bernhagen

I made Cursillo #1 in our state in July of 1978. I tell you this because like many of you, Cursillo has had a major impact on our lives and has challenged us in our own ways to be Evangelizers for Christ or to "bloom where we are planted."

After my weekend, I quickly found a reunion group and have been grouping ever since. My group was asked to work Cursillo #2 since there were still slim pickings of people to work on a Cursillo Weekend team. We were also asked to work multiple jobs. Kay Brown, the Rectora for Cursillo #1 and #2, told me that one of my jobs was music director. I looked at her like she had lost her mind, but I also knew my response had to be, "How high?"

She further explained I had to learn the song Hosea on the guitar for the weekend. That was all well and good, except for a couple of things: one, I didn't even own a guitar and two, I didn't know how to play one. This new challenge and my yes to God, was the start of an incredible journey for me.

I did learn to play Hosea with its 3 chords for Cursillo #2. It was not pretty. I also played the other songs we sang, using only the three chords I knew. There were many gaps where everyone kept singing, and I had to catch up with the guitar chords.

This was the start of living out my Fourth Day. I began to learn more chords and continued to work Cursillo teams. Through much prayer (Piety) and lots of chord books and playing with records (Study), I knew that playing for Cursillo was God's calling for me. (Action)

God gave me the gift of music to share and to bring others to Christ through sung prayer. It was not pretty at first, but God used me as His instrument, and He still does today through my music and my guitar.

I not only played for Cursillo, but I also began playing for my church, Our Lady of the Hills, alongside three other guitar players. Next thing I knew, I was the only one left because they all moved away. Once again, I found myself in the position of learning chords and praying God would lead, guide, and show me the way.

He showed me the way alright! God has a sense of humor as, next thing I knew, I was the director of our church's Joyful Noise choir. By this time, I was more mature in my Christian journey, and I knew the first thing I needed to do with this group was bring in prayer. So, before each practice and mass, we started praying that God would use us as His instrument. We would ask Him to send down the Holy Spirit that the words we were about to sing may be His words. We started offering prayers and petitions for each other. With God at my side, He helped me grow our choir from a bunch of individuals to a Christian Community working to sing praise to our Father.

We started learning about the songs we were singing and why that song was chosen. We learned that when we sing, we assist members of our congregation in *their* prayer. We learned about our roles as music ministers and how important our role is. As the leader, it was my job to teach our group why we sing and who we sing for. It is not for our glory but to bring the people in the pews to Christ through our communal sung prayer!

Eventually we expanded our Evangelization by bringing church to those who physically could not come to church. We would bring Communion and our songs of prayer to the shut-ins of our parish. We went to nursing homes, assisted living, sang at funeral homes and anywhere God called us to sing His praise. With the onset of COVID, we began livestreaming our 5:30 vigil mass for those who could not come in person, and we continue doing that to this day. Our mission was and is to bring others closer to God through sung prayer.

Just think all of this started through Cursillo. I answered my YES to God's call by learning how to play the guitar, and now I use that gift, not only with Cursillo, but at my parish and beyond. How is God calling you to serve? What will your answer be?

MY REFLECTION _______________________________________

____

____

Led by God
Mike Solly

My journey with Cursillo began amidst the snowy landscape of the Finger Lakes region in New York, as I trudged alone to Sunday mass at my Episcopal college. With a yearning for a deeper connection to my faith, I pondered, "Surely, the Church has more to offer me." Little did I know that this pursuit to draw closer to God would lead me to the transformative path of Cursillo, a movement that significantly altered the course of my life.

It wasn't until I reached the age of 62 that I discovered Cursillo and its profound impact. This spiritual journey awakened me to the gifts bestowed upon me by God and ignited within me a fervor to utilize these gifts in His service. Before experiencing my own Cursillo weekend, I noticed the absence of a men's Cursillo reunion group in our parish. This realization kindled a calling within me to initiate not just one, but two men's Cursillo Groups in 2008 and 2010 respectively, both of which continue to thrive today.

My leadership capabilities found their purpose as I took the helm as Rector for weekend number 60 and served diligently on the diocesan Cursillo Secretariat. Additionally, I played a pivotal role in leading our deanery school of leaders and ultreya at various times. Despite my proficiency in public speaking, initially rooted in a career in finance, I found Cursillo to be much more than mere study during my weekend. It uncovered deeper layers of spiritual growth and understanding that went beyond academia.

Cursillo revolutionized my approach to evangelization. Before this journey, I had seldom vocalized my faith. Now, I actively seek opportunities daily to share my beliefs, utilizing my God-given talent for public speaking to lector at church and guide friends towards Christ. Furthermore, I've had the privilege of sponsoring numerous Cursillistas.I have used my financial acumen to lead the parish finance council for 15 years.

In essence, my voyage with Cursillo has been an enriching odyssey that unveiled not only my spiritual potential but also my capacity for leadership, evangelism, and service to both God and his Church.

MY REFLECTION ____

____

____

Almost Perfect Love Story
Sharon Shymansky Roberts

Thy will be done. It is not for us to question why or to know the answer. As Christians we are asked to accept His will, to give Him our love, to thank and praise Him, and to believe in His wisdom, thus strengthening our faith, even in troubled times.

Every woman dreams of her perfect love story. Handsome fiancé, beautiful wedding, devoted husband, wonderful kids. All that and much more had been mine. And then, one day, the marriage ended.

The first hint that the marriage might end came one day in the hospital lobby where I was waiting for my husband, David, to get out of surgery. He was having a lump removed that was visible under his ear and extended to his jawline. He wasn't overly concerned. Doctors and our dentist had examined him and no one had raised any red flags, at least not to me. This was simply a procedure to remove the nuisance of a cyst. Our 22-year-old son, DJ, was waiting with me in the hospital's family waiting room. The wait had already been lengthy, and I admit I was getting a little nervous.

The doctor was upon me before I even noticed his entrance. He motioned me to a table and we sat down. "Mrs. Shymansky, I'll be honest. It doesn't look good. We've taken a sample of the cyst and are sending it out for a biopsy. I'm going to admit David overnight for observation. I'll have the biopsy report in the morning, and then all of us will sit down and talk. I'm going to make the arrangements to have him admitted. You can spend the night here with him. Someone will come and get you soon. I'll see you in the morning." With a pat on my hand, he was gone. Never had the C word been mentioned, but it loomed large in my brain.

I am ashamed to admit that I went into shock. I crawled into my son's lap and began crying. I've lived with that shame all this time, and I am telling you now, DJ, how sorry I am that I wasn't stronger for *you* at that moment. In my defense, I was appalled that cancer could possibly find its way into my Marine Corps, police officer, husband. 6 foot 6 ½ inches, 250-pound handsome hunks who never smoked do NOT get cancer, even if they did serve two tours of duty in Vietnam, where the use of Agent Orange was prevalent. Loving husbands and incredible fathers who have been happily married for 24 years do not suddenly get cancer. This wasn't possible.

In the next few moments, I did two things. I did what every daughter does when she's troubled; I called my mom and told her what the doctor had said. Then I went to the hospital chapel, fell to my knees, and prayed. "Please Lord, hear my prayer! Lord, I know that your will be done, but if you could allow this disease to pass us by, I would be forever grateful."

That didn't happen. I spent the night in the hospital with David, and in the morning we got the news from the doctor. "I got the lab report back on the biopsy, and it isn't good news. It's squamous cell carcinoma, the cancer that infects soft tissue. It apparently began at the base of your tongue, David, and progressed from there. We believe it has invaded the lymph nodes in your neck, but we are going to do exploratory surgery to see just how extensive the invasion has been. We'll take the infected lymph nodes out. But first, we're going to set you up for radiation treatments for the next four weeks. We might shrink the cancer that way. You should know, David, cancer comes in stages. The stages identify how far the cancer has likely progressed. Your cancer is stage IV."

David spoke for the first time. "How bad is stage IV?"

The doctor looked directly at David when he answered. "It's the worst. It means the cancer has spread significantly from the original site."

This was worse news than either of us had anticipated. We reached for each other's hands at the same moment, each of us searching for strength from the other. "Okay, then. I guess we have a fight on our hands, and I hope you're up to the challenge!" was David's only response.

The drive home was quiet, each of us deep in thought as we attempted to digest the devastating news. I remember silently praying on the ride home for David's full recovery from the disease, and for strength for us both as he began the journey back to good health. Since God had seen fit to allow the cancer to happen, perhaps He would allow David to recover. We were certainly going to do our part!

But God chose not to answer that prayer, either. David fought with every ounce of his being. over the next 26 months, but the onslaught into his soft tissue continued and grew despite two radiation treatments a day for several weeks and many, many months of chemotherapy. The cancer would disappear in one place, only to reappear somewhere else. Finally, it invaded his lungs. After all the treatments, my husband was a weakened shell, falling to just above 90 pounds. Through it all, our sons, myself, his sister, brother, sister-in-law, my sister and my mom became caretakers, watching over him, praying for him, making him comfortable, but the day came when he realized that the battle was almost over, and that he had lost.

I remember it well. The cancer doctor told me that morning that, in his opinion, David had less than a month to live, but I had just been told by our new oncologist that he wanted David to start a new round of chemotherapy! I shared that news with the doctor and, between the sobs, told him I didn't want David to pass sick from chemotherapy. If he was about to die, I wanted him to have a chance to rest and pass in peace. The doctor agreed that further treatment was unnecessary and was kind enough to contact hospice for me. That afternoon, I told David that a nurse would be coming to help us so that he wouldn't have to go through all the fuss, bother, and pain of dressing for doctor visits and riding to the doctor's office. The doctor would be coming to us from now on until he got stronger. His job was to rest, eat, and begin building himself back up.

That evening he dragged himself into the bathroom. I was never very far and when he whispered my name, I was there. He was standing before the mirror, looking at himself. "I'm dying, aren't I?"

In the moment, my heart broke, and though it has been 24 years since his death, it has never fully healed. "Why would you say that, David? You're no worse than you have been. You just need to eat more and rest to get your strength back. Your doctor doesn't want you exerting yourself any more than you have to."

He stared intently at me and then shuffled silently to the bed. Later that night, when I was wrapped snugly in his arms, he whispered, "I'm not ready to leave you. I love you so much."

"Then keep fighting! I need you and love you. You're my hero, my husband, and my best friend. That's a hole too big to leave me with! Just get better and stay with me."

"I want to, honey, but I don't think I can. I'm tired, really tired."

In the ensuing days, the hospice nurse began her routine, visiting every other day. The doctor came once a week. David was put on oxygen 24/7, his morphine was increased, and every day he spent a bit more time sleeping. He was getting ready for death; I was getting ready for a miracle. Every day found me praying, "Please, God, let David get his appetite back today." "Please God, let David have a pain-free day." "Please God, let David feel stronger today." None of those things happened, and you would think that I would be angry at God for refusing to answer any of my prayers. But strangely enough, above all else, each day found me grateful to Him for giving me one more day with the man I loved. I realized, eventually, that David was going on a journey, one he had prepared for all his life. How could I be unhappy when I knew that David was going to heaven and would spend eternity with the Lord? Isn't that what every Christian lives for? That thought kept me strong and helped me survive the loss I was about to experience.

One evening, two of our sons, DJ and Cory, and David's sister, brother and sister-in-law were all sitting with me in our bedroom. David had been sleeping most of the evening. Suddenly, he was wide awake and pointing towards the window. "Turn out the light," he spoke in a weak, raspy voice. "It's too bright! It's hurting my eyes!" Even though it was nighttime, and there was no light on in the bedroom except the tiny lamp at the bedside, we all turned and looked at the window. As expected, there was no light coming through the closed blinds, not even a hint. David was sitting up now, his arm shielding his eyes. "Please, please go away. Make the light go away," he spoke in an anguished voice, and then he fell back onto the bed and into a deep sleep. I'm not certain what the others thought, but I am convinced the Angels came for David that night. He didn't go willingly, though, because he was still with us the next morning, though he was barely breathing and unresponsive. However, at 6:09 AM, the exact birth time of his oldest son, David exhaled his final breath and our marriage ended.

To say I was brokenhearted is an understatement. The moment he took his final breath, I began missing him. I miss him still. But even in the throes of the anguish and heartbreak, there was a deeper feeling inside me. There was joy. It wasn't joy for me; it was joy for David. For 26 months, I had watched him suffer. I had witnessed his pain, his grief, his frustration, and finally, his acceptance. Now, he was beyond all that. His only experience for the rest of eternity would be one of joy so beautiful and bountiful, the human mind is incapable of imagining it, and for that I was grateful. I was grateful that his mother had introduced him to the Lord. I was grateful that he had experienced a personal relationship with the Lord as he was growing into that brave, honorable, loving man. And I was thankful and humbled that God had chosen me to be David's partner.

Though we didn't have a lifetime together the way a perfect love story would, the time we did have was a blessing. So, how could I be angry at God? God's will had been done, and my job was to seek comfort from Him and continue to thank Him every day of my life for having loaned David to me in the first place. My life is richer and more blessed for having been his wife.

MY REFLECTION ____

____

____

Chapter Eighteen

Christianity in Action

Christianity in Action Summary
Sharon Shymansky Roberts

We doubt there is a single person alive who will dispute the message of this rollo - *people need people*. However, it may be that by the time you got to this talk on Sunday afternoon, you were already in an exhaustive state, or in shell shock, or both. And that would have been a shame because the Christianity in Action rollo complements the Study of the Environment rollo you heard just before this one. Where Study of the Environment explained the battlefield and the strategies needed to win your environments to Christ, this rollo was the "how to."

In the Study of the Environment rollo we saw, in theory, how to strategically conquer each of our environments and evangelize. That was scary! Evangelize? That word may have frightened you. "No way," your inner self shouted! By now, though, you know that is exactly what Christ is asking each of us to do. So, together we opened this box, Christianity in Action, and the Cursillista who shared it showed you, through personal testimonies, how easy it can be to change your environments to Christ. She/He demonstrated how a Christian acts and thinks and how, by his/her very presence, an environment can be changed. And where did that change begin for him or her? It began with a small group of like-minded Cursillistas with whom she/he meets weekly.

Let's review the definition of Christianity in Action you learned in this rollo. *Christianity in Action is a **group** of **Grace-filled Christians** who **live together** in a **climate** that makes it possible for each one to **live** and **spread the Gospel** in the world.*

Notice the words that are in bold letters. Let us focus on them. **Group**. We hope by now you understand that word because you are already in a weekly reunion group. But just in case you aren't, let's look at what a friendship or reunion group is. It is small, with maybe four to six members. You meet weekly in the same place at the same time. All are committed to being there and seldom miss meetings. But what makes them a group and not just a collection of people?

First, through meeting as a group, they have become close friends and know one another well. Through that knowledge, a true admiration for one another has grown. They recognize that all of them are on the same journey to Christ, though their paths may have differed.

Second, all are **Grace-filled Christians.** Each member lives his/her ordinary life in God's grace 24 hours a day, seven days a week. His/her focus is always on the Lord and serving Him in any way He asks is their mission. They execute that mission joyfully, as they understand they are doing His work and are proud to have been called to it!

Third, they **"live together,"** each time they meet, in a **climate** blessed by the Holy Spirit. All members accepted the challenge of continuing to grow in knowing Him by reading, listening to one another, developing an effective prayer routine, and being attentive in Mass. They bring that knowledge and growth with them each time they meet, and they share what it has done for them.

Finally, they all actively live their Christianity – they **spread the Gospel**. They evangelize. They share their evangelization efforts, successes, and failures honestly in their group and are uplifted by the encouragement and counsel of its members.

Because of this small group of brothers or sisters in Christ, and the courage and conviction they impart to you (and you to them), you can stand firm in your faith, no matter the circumstance. People need people!

MY REFLECTION ____

____

____

A New Way
Theresa Marie

I never knew how much of a control freak I was until my Cursillo weekend. I remember being in adoration late Saturday night during my weekend and thinking, "Ok, God, I am sitting here with you. It's just me and you. Send me your message. What am I supposed to be getting out of this weekend?" I sat by myself thinking how I was the only one up and sitting in adoration. Surely, God will speak to me. Ten minutes, 15 minutes, 30 minutes go by, and I was still sitting and waiting for some revelation. I was frustrated, as I knew the next day was the end of the weekend and time was running out for me to receive my message.

I mean, how pompous of me to assume that God would provide a message to me on MY time. I mean…I was being good. I was up spending time with Jesus instead of sleeping. It is funny and humbling to look back and "see" my thoughts and expectations. Always wanting things in MY time.

God's message for me hit me like a ton of bricks Sunday during the Christianity in Action talk, whose message is "People need People." I have lived my life totally in control, at least I thought so. I didn't need people. I needed to protect myself *from* people. During the talk, I began crying, and I sobbed so hard, I could not even speak after hearing that talk. My entire table surrounded me, hugged me, and loved on me while I released all the control to God. A beautiful woman at my table had brought out a Divine Mercy image that day and she faced Jesus towards me. The words, "Jesus, I trust in you" stared back at me.

You see, I trusted in myself. I trusted that I could control what people might think of me. I hid the flaws in my life. I only wanted people to see the best of me. I hid my flaw so that people would never think I had failed as a mother. How could this Catholic woman, whose husband is a deacon, have a son that is gay? What I wanted to hide even more was that my son no longer believes in God. I must have messed up somewhere down the road. I wanted God to convert my son quickly so that I didn't have any explaining to do. Please God, please change his heart, and change it right now! Look at me trying to control things I had no control over.

What I realized that weekend was that I could no longer do things my way. I had no control over what people might think or say about me or my family. That was for God to deal with. All I knew was that I needed people. I needed people that loved God, saw me, and loved me despite the dirty and not so pretty things in my life. I needed people to pray for me, see the real me, and listen to my real-life struggles. I also needed people to love, to pray for, and to be a friend to.

I shared about my son at an Ultreya. It was so difficult for me to share the things I didn't want people to see. My wounds were raw and open, but this new family of friends listened and passed no judgment. They cried with me and thanked me for sharing so openly. Many shared their own struggles with children and families.

It was surely no coincidence that my Cursillo table saint was Saint Monica, the mother of St. Augustine. I didn't know who she was at the time, but later I learned that she spent her life praying for her son's conversion. She shed many tears and was steadfast in her prayers. I wear a St. Monica bracelet every day to remind me that, with Jesus, there is hope. St. Monica, pray for us. Jesus, I trust in You.

MY REFLECTION ____

____

____

Just Smile
Andrea Marcella

When I was young, I remember seeing a poster with a boy carrying another boy on his shoulders. The slogan was, "He's not heavy, he's my brother." That slogan was the symbol of Boys Town. What better love than helping our brothers and sisters in small ways? Maybe not carrying them physically on our shoulders but helping them in times of trouble or stress.

Sometimes, just a smile or a hug can work wonders. I remember when I worked as a teller in a bank. There was one lady who came into the bank on a regular basis. She was very difficult to please so, when we saw her coming, most of the tellers pretended to be busy or actually left their stations. I felt so badly for this poor woman. She deserved better than to be ignored. I always greeted her with a smile and asked how she was doing. Usually, she ignored my question.

One day she came in and it looked to me like she had been crying. When she came to my window, I greeted her as usual, but this time she told me that her beloved dog had died. She said she knew people would think she was silly being so upset over an animal, but her dog was the only thing she had in her life that made her happy. My heart broke for her. She then went on to say she had appreciated that I was always kind to an old lady and that she liked to come into the bank because I always greeted her with a smile.

Just one smile can make all the difference in a person's day!

MY REFLECTION ____

____

____

My Birthday Card Ministry
Nancy Szarowicz

I'm not quite sure if I remember exactly how or why I started this ministry. I know that Wilma Irvin was the one doing it first, and I remember I started it before she passed away. In fact, I do recall back in maybe 2018, during the Lenten season, I listened to a podcast of Father Mike Schmidt where he recommended his listeners think of 40 people that have touched their lives and write them a thank you note. I very much enjoy writing and penmanship. I loved learning it in school and practiced nonstop. In addition to that, I enjoyed teaching cursive to second and third graders. So, I was ready to write!

What really sticks in my mind is that I began this ministry as an action for my Cursillo group. I think I started doing this ministry in 2021. Each week I look at the birthday listings in the church bulletin to see who I know. Then I may a list of all the names. I normally go weekly or biweekly to the dollar store to buy my cards. I choose the religious ones that make me feel good, and I hope they will touch them as well. At times, I order a set from Amazon. I select a time and sit and write out short birthday messages, personalized for each recipient if I can.

I feel very content as I am writing out these notes, and I ponder carefully about the people that I am sending them to. I send them because I think everyone likes to receive personal, handwritten mail since we receive so many emails these days. I know I love getting handwritten notes!

As far as living out my fourth day, I never thought about it that way, but we did learn, during our Cursillo weekend, to "Bloom where you are planted." I feel I am planted and still blooming in my church, since I have belonged to it since its beginning, and it is so dear to me. I consider the people I know very dear, too.

And so, each week I write these cards. I know these cards have touched many peoples' hearts because I have received countless thanks through cards, words, and hugs. Just this past week, a young woman ran up to me and gave me the longest and most heartfelt hug ever. She told me how much she appreciated the gesture. I am now collecting many precious thank you cards, but this ministry is not about me; it's about letting each person know I am glad God gave them life and brought them into my "square meter."

MY REFLECTION ______________________________________

____

____

Christianity in Action
Marianne Joy

In the Action Rollo, we heard about two distinct aspects of Christianity in Action. There's Christian Action, and there's Apostolic Action.

One day I was in the checkout line at Walmart, and as I was putting my groceries on the conveyor belt, I noticed that the man behind me was in one of those motorized carts. He was an elderly gentleman, and he wore a Navy cap on his head. His little basket was full of stuff and I asked him if he would like me to put his items on the belt for him. I think he was a little taken aback at first. Probably nobody ever asked him if they could do that for him before. So I started putting his produce and his boxes and whatever he had on the conveyor belt. He thanked me. Looking at his cap, I told him that my daddy was a World War II Army veteran.

We had a conversation about my dad, and it turned out that he was born the same year as my dad, who would have been 97 had he lived. I told him that Daddy's motto was, "If I can't help you, I would never do anything to hurt you." Anyway, he told me that my dad taught me well. It was a brief exchange, and such a simple thing, but I'm pretty sure it brightened his day. That's Christian action. Jesus told us the 2nd greatest commandment was to love our neighbor…

Apostolic action goes a step further. We share our faith with others in order that they may desire a relationship with Christ. After the last Women's Weekend, we all got together at Saint Bernard's Church for a group reunion. While we were there, it so happened that the Girl Scouts were also meeting at the church. The Girl Scout leader asked if some of the girls could join us and if we could teach them how to pray the Rosary. It was so beautiful. We explained to them what we were going to do, and a few of the girls were selected to lead in the decades.

Time passed, and one day I received an email from Saint Bernard's that the Girl Scouts were going to meet again and they wanted to know whether they could pray the Rosary with us again. It had been about a year and a half, but they obviously never forgot it, and they wanted to do it again. So, we made ararranged for them to meet us. We went into the chapel, and we prayed with them.

After we finished praying the Rosary, the other Cursillistas left, but I stayed behind to talk to the girls. I explained to them that we need to meditate on the mysteries. I told them, when I pray at home, I put myself into the scene and I imagine that I'm having a conversation with the Blessed Mother. And I gave them this example. The first Joyful Mystery that we prayed was the Annunciation. And I imagine the angel Gabriel appearing to Mary and telling her that she will conceive and bear a child, and Mary is like, how can this be? For she was consecrated to the Lord. And the angel told her that the Holy Spirit would overshadow her and she would conceive. Look at Elizabeth, who in her old age is with child, and they called her barren. For with God all things are possible. And Mary said, "Let it be done to me according to your word."

The girls looked at me as I was talking, taking it all in. We must have made an impact on them if a year and a half later they wanted to pray with us again! We should do everything we can to reach our young people and lead them to a closer relationship with our Lord, starting when they are young. I can only pray that they will walk closely with Christ throughout their life's journey.

Christianity in Action is a group of Grace filled Christians who journey together in a climate that makes it possible for each one to live and spread the gospel in the world.

In December 2018, Bishop James Checchio in my Diocese of Metuchen, NJ proclaimed a year of preparation for consecration of our diocese to Our Lady of Guadalupe. The Diocese planned several events and, as a result, I participated in some powerful groups of grace-filled Christians in Action.

In September 2019, I was blessed to go on the 9 mile Walking Pilgrimage through the streets, hills, and fields of beautiful rural Hunterdon County, NJ. It was called "The Way of Saint Juan Diego", who had walked nine miles regularly to attend Mass and receive religious instruction, which led him to enter the Catholic Church in 1524. There were more than 700 of us walking that day! The Holy Spirit filled our hearts and the air was full of excitement as we sang, prayed and praised our God. On the last break, we participated in a Holy Hour outdoors in a park in High Bridge. Newly ordained Fr. Michael Tabernero led us in prayer, along with Fr. Tim Christy, Vicar General for the Diocese of Metuchen.

Afterward, Fr. Tim led the Eucharistic Procession for the last three miles of our pilgrimage, and Bishop Checchio walked with us. Jesus led the way! As we left the park, we sang the Divine Mercy prayer.

There were visitors in the park who were not in our group and they stared in wonder as we filed past them, worshipping and singing. It was extremely powerful and I will never forget that day! To this day, I still say that it was one of the best days of my life!

I also went to the Basilica of Our Lady of Guadalupe in Mexico City with Bishop Checchio the following month. Seeing the tilma of Our Lady of Guadalupe right in front of my eyes was a dream come true. This time there were 78 pilgrims.

And you know, over ten percent of those on pilgrimage were Cursillistas! Three priests, a deacon and five laypersons, all Cursillistas. There is a camaraderie in a group such as this… as we journeyed together for five days, praying and worshipping together, sharing meals and sharing our faiths with new friends - all of us with a common bond – Jesus!

MY REFLECTION ____

____

____

Chapter Nineteen

Cursillista Beyond the Cursillo

Cursillista Beyond the Cursillo Summary
Sharon Shymansky Roberts

Perhaps you arrived Thursday anxious and concerned. Maybe you were even a bit defiant at being kidnapped and transported to a parish center hours away from your home, with nothing but a suitcase and bedding! Or maybe you arrived in eager anticipation of growing closer to Christ. Whatever state-of-mind you arrived in, you likely did not expect a mission directly from Christ, but that is exactly what happened. You soon learned you were called there to help bring others to Him, to encourage, convince, and enthuse others *for* Him. As Cursillistas, we cannot rest until the entire world knows and loves Him and feels as alive and joyful as you did on the last day of your weekend.

That mission may have seemed impossible at the time until you became aware that an abundance of Grace had been given to you through your participation that weekend. You came to know that it would be His Grace that would help you accomplish His mission. You learned that His Grace is abundant in your daily life as well. When you spend alone time with Him, you receive His Grace. When you attend mass, you receive His Grace. When you accept the Eucharist, knowing you are accepting Him into your body, you receive His Grace. In every sacrament, you receive His Grace. He hasn't left you without the tools you need to accomplish your mission; He has supplied them abundantly.

Speaking of tools…You were given a "tripod of tools" to help you accomplish your mission. Piety. Study. Action. These tools not only help you tackle Christ's mission you have now been given, but they are the foundation of how to move *yourself* closer to Christ. All three legs need to be developed within you constantly. The direction of your whole life must point toward God. These tools help you do that. Remember, you cannot love what you do not know. Your mission, put simply, is to make a friend, be a friend, and bring that friend to Christ.

You were warned, however, to be aware of two dangers as you began performing this mission – lack of humility and lack of confidence. To combat a lack of humility, one needs only to remember that we are only *instruments* of the Lord and, as His instruments, He is always using us. It's not all about us and what WE can do; it's about Him and what He DOES through us! If you lack confidence, you were asked to have confidence in HIS plan, not yours. With Christ, we can do all things! Remember Galatians, Chapter 2:20: ..." Yet I live, no longer I, but Christ lives in me..." Therefore, the solution to the two dangers, you were told, was to stay in contact with Christ and continue the journey through constant contact with your Grace-filled brothers and sisters.

What did you develop within you that weekend to help you on your mission? You now had a clear ideal. Your eyes were focused on Jesus, and you realized you were supported in the strength of Christ. Therefore, you left your weekend with a heart equipped to bring the life of Christ and the news of salvation to your environments of family, friends, work, and play. You learned that apostolic potential is not the same in everyone. Remember, no one can do everything, but everyone can do something. Because we are different, and created with different potentials and talents, we accomplish our mission in different ways, but we all have the same purpose – to build up Christ's kingdom.

You were made aware of the vital importance of encouraging and enthusing one another when you regularly meet in Group Reunion. By sharing your piety, study, apostolic actions, close moments, successes, and failures, you increase one another's awareness of your lives in Grace. Thus, together you grow in your ability to effectively spread the Good News through apostolic action.

You left your weekend with a clear mission. You left equipped through His Grace to perform it effectively and continuously as you lived your Fourth Day. Are you carrying out your mission?

MY REFLECTION _________________________________

____

____

Hungry and Grateful
Sarah Ingram

I was in Charleston dog-sitting for a friend. Every week she and her husband get a box of vegetables through their local CSA. Since they were gone for several weeks, she asked me to get the box every week and told me to eat whatever I wanted. Fantastic! Being five months pregnant, I need all the vegetables I can get. The problem is that the box is for two people for a week, and while I'm eating for two, I'm not eating THAT MUCH. I ended up not being able to finish the first box before I had to get the second one. I knew I wasn't going to be able to make a dent in the second box, so I resolved I would take the vegetables to my mom who is on a restricted income.

As I drive to my mom's, I must take some busy highways, including 526. As I'm driving along, I'm excited to give this food to someone who could really use it. I take my exit, and, on the side of the road, I see a gentleman with a sign. "Not homeless, just don't have food. Anything would be appreciated." Whelp! Ok, Lord. I'm listening. Literally sent me a physical sign. Appreciate that. I pull over on the shoulder and stop beside him.

I roll down my window and ask if he has a way to cook food. He says, "Yes, ma'am, I do." I'm so excited to get rid of this extra box of food so it doesn't go to waste that I quickly get out of my car! But my pregnancy brain isn't working, and I forget to put the car in park. I quickly correct my mistake. I then get out on the side of the interstate exit to grab the box from the back of my car. The light turns green, and I hurriedly say to the man, "I'm so sorry I don't have more for you and I can't stay! I hope you can use this!" I hand him the box, which he accepts gratefully. I drive off, feeling very proud of myself and how I clearly just listened to God's call.

I'm a little late to meet my mom, but that's ok. As I drive, I realize that I need to return the box I just gave away back to the CSA. That's how it works, you see. Each week you drop off your old box and pick up the new box with your new vegetables. And I just gave someone else's box (with their name and address, mind you) to a stranger on the street! Maybe I could call the CSA and explain? Maybe I could offer to buy another box? Or maybe I could just swing back by later and grab the box if he's still out there? I resolve to do that. I'll get some plastic grocery bags and swap out the box for the bags, assuming he's still there.

I spend the afternoon with my mom. As I begin my drive back to the dog-sitting gig, I pray the man is still out there, and that I get the box back. I've got some grocery bags at the ready. I'm nearing the exit and it dawns on me that there isn't really a suitable place to pull over except the "median" (if you can call it that) between the six lanes of traffic. Oh well! Holy Spirit, help! Protect me! I see the gentleman still standing there with his sign, the box behind him. I pull over into the median, put the car in park (I **can** learn), and put the flashers on. The light is about to change, so I run across traffic with my grocery bags to get to him. (My husband was not very happy when I told him this part of the story.) I shout out to him so I don't surprise him. He turns with a smile on his face and greets me. I say, "I'm so sorry to barge in on you. Do you remember me? I gave you the box of vegetables just a few hours ago."

"Yes, ma'am!" he replies. "Hard to forget a pregnant lady who forgot to put her car in park." We both smile and I already know I like this guy. I introduce myself. He says his name is Charles. I explain the story about the box and if he'd be ok if I swapped out the box for the bags I brought. He's totally fine with this.

I crouch down and start to move the food to the bags. He tells me this is the craziest interaction he's had on the side of the road, and then he insists that I stop crouching and let him move the food. Then I see it. This man has already taken the tomatoes out, cut them up with a plastic knife and the pieces are resting on a piece of broken Tupperware. He was clearly hungry, and he'd been standing on the side of the road in blessed Charleston heat the entire time I was inside visiting with my mother in the air conditioning. My heart breaks for him. Turns out we really should trust people when they say they're hungry.

Charles and I make small talk as we're swapping food vessels. We're about to part ways when he says, "God bless you, ma'am." I take this as another sign. I ask Charles what else he needs, what else I can pray for. I explain I'm only in town for a little bit, but I'd be happy to pray for him at Mass. He says he's grateful for the prayers and just hopes he can continue to get enough food for him and his wife. He says he's very grateful for the vegetables. Then HE asks ME how he can pray for me! I tell him just to pray for the safety and health of our little one as this is our first pregnancy. He smiles and we both promise to pray for each other. We leave with a friendly handshake and a common knowledge we're both trying to follow Christ.

I get back to my car with my empty box, successfully weaving through the onramp of interstate traffic. I realize I could have just given Charles the food-- but anyone can do that. The difference between action and apostolic action is bringing Christ along with you. And even though

I thought I was the one doing the good deed, Charles showed me that Christ can be found anywhere, even between two strangers on the street swapping vegetables from boxes to bags.

MY REFLECTION ____

____

____

Cursillo, My Passion!
Maria del Carmen Beltran

Hello, how are my brothers and sisters in Christ doing? I have been living my Cursillo of Christianity since July 7 to 10, 2016 in NC. I am a mother of two beautiful daughters that God let me borrow, and I serve in the church of Our Lady Star of the Sea, North Myrtle Beach, SC. I want to share a little about my fourth day as I am living it.

I received several invitations to attend a Cursillo weekend from others, but I did not listen until my sponsor, José Guadalupe Landa (may he rest in peace) convinced me to attend. I accepted his invitation to live the Cursillo. From that day on, my life changed totally. Before, I lived to work and have material things, often forgetting my family and not attending Mass. I learned that God must be first, and I learned to value myself as a woman, love my family and my neighbor. My life is full of challenges and struggles, but they give me the strength to continue persevering and following the way of the Lord.

It has not been easy, but the struggles I have made me fall in love more with the Lord My God and the Cursillo of Christianity Movement. Getting to know that God loves me and that my brothers and sisters are here to help me is life changing. Now, I serve in my parish as an extraordinary minister of the Holy Eucharist. I remember the first time I gave the Eucharist; I was very nervous but also very happy and appreciative of serving Christ.

We now have a School of Leaders, since our brothers and sisters of the Diocese of Raleigh adopted us. We also have the Ultreya and a friendship group. Most recently, I thank God for putting an Angel in my path, Ms. Annie Ortiz, who is helping us a lot in SC to begin the Cursillos in Spanish.

My passion is to bring many more souls to Christ so that they can live what I am living, knowing that God loves us. When I first attended Our Lady Star of the Sea, I was the only Cursillista. At that time, I decided to invite men and women to attend Ultreyas at St. Breden in Charlotte, NC. They started realizing that they too wanted to live what I had already lived, the Cursillo. As of today, I have sponsored five men and six women with the support of a Priest named Fr. Cirilo Bailon, who was the Vicar.

MY REFLECTION ____

____

____

Eulogy for Thomas John Callan, Jr.
Deacon James Chin

Crying - It's a beautiful thing. When we cry, it is all the unexpressed Love, the Grief that will remain with us, until we pass because we never get enough time with each other … No matter if someone lives till 10, 75, or 100.. this grief stays with us because it's the unexpressed Love that we never got to say. We all told Tom every day how much he was our best friend, the best dad, the best husband. But in the end, there is never enough time on this earth to express how much we love a person when we Love like God.

I am indeed honored to convey this incredible life of Major Thomas John Callan, but make no mistake, this Eulogy is a combined effort of the memories of his group of praying brothers, his Catholic community at Our Lady of the Lake, and his family. I am simply an instrument of Tom's Spirit through Jesus Christ, conveying the life that he shared through prayers, kind thoughts, and actions, which enabled everyone he encountered to live a better life.

After the football game last week, on the night of his death, he expressed his love to Ursula and thanked her for another beautiful day because of her. Those were his last words. We know so well the last few days of his life because Tom Callan was not shy about sharing his thoughts and feelings. We know that he began the weekend by going to daily mass on the first Friday of the month, a tradition his mom taught him long ago and one where he discovered the beauty of God's presence. We know he adored the Blessed Sacrament that evening in our adoration chapel and participated in Holy Benediction. On Saturday, we know he went to the "Right to Life March" to do what he could to protect and save the lives of babies that he viewed as God's innocent creations. On Sunday, we know that he was excited to help a friend by being the Lector at Mass.

We know all this because, on Monday morning, Tom Callan shared his extraordinary weekend with his Cursillo brothers. He was happy and felt connected with God. We all have grown to love this man whose persona was larger than life, but on that Monday, he glowed. Tom had shaved his beard for the New Year and he wanted to impress Ursula with his good looks. When we asked him why he had shaved, his answer was simply to make Ursula happy and, besides, it was time to start looking the part of how he felt. We could all sense something was different about him. Maybe not his positive usual self, but happier and more peaceful. He wanted to make a special prayer for our brother, Alex Ciani, who passed last year to COVID. Tom wanted us to remember Alex, our brother, who had done so much with children for God.

For Tom, meeting every Monday morning was an important bond he cherished. That came from his Marine tradition of "Sempre Fe." Regardless, we are indebted to Christ for connecting us with Tom whose life was about serving others above himself, to serve his God on the Altar in any way he could. For Tom, his life was one about living the Beatitudes we heard today in the Gospel.

So how do we honor a man known to be "larger than life!" This statement has both a literal, spiritual, and physical metaphor when you think about it. Tom joined our Cursillo Monday morning prayer group in 2018 with the purpose of "improving his understanding of his faith and getting closer to God". Each Monday morning, we broke bread, shared our weekly encounters with God, prayed, and supported each other in a bond endearing to our souls. Our friendship, Our Band of Brothers, grew over time that has cultivated a Love that has formed us closer to Christ. During his brief but priceless time of bonding, we learned much about one another. Tom was a man whose accolades certainly dwarf those of many of us, especially mine. But behind his daunting physical presence and career successes, you discover a humble, selfless, and devoted man whose principal focus centered on God, Family, and Country.

For example, on the feast day of St. Thomas, Tom reminded everyone that St. Thomas was his patron saint for the very reason St. Thomas is known for.. his doubt. As an Irish Catholic growing up in New York and losing his father at an early age, he learned much from his Catholic Faith from his mom and his Church. Tom was proud of his Irish heritage and serving as an Altar Boy at St. Patrick's Cathedral, especially when his favored uncle was ordained a priest there. As a young adult attending Villanova University, an Augustinian Catholic University, I joked with Tom that despite his Augustinian and Military training, he had the heart of St. Francis. Like St. Thomas, Tom admitted to being skeptical about things and always questioning everything. I believe his inquiring childlike mind helped him discover God throughout his life. He discovered God in everything good and beautiful. Often he would say how he would see beauty in all of God's creation, such as walking the Palmetto Trails, working at Harvest Hope, and just meeting people. One morning when he came for breakfast, he looked all bruised and beat up and we jokingly asked him how the other guy looked. He said he lost the fight to a tree. "A tree we asked?" and he said that he had tripped on the Palmetto Trail and the tree got in his way. Soon afterward, Tom had us pray for that tree.

Since 2018, Tom took an interest in studying about God, which included picking my brain and Deacon Malcolm's on his porch while sipping Bourbon spirits. He was one to always share his enlightening discovery with everyone like an excited young boy. For example, when he learned that I was studying Aquinas' Summa Theologica, Tom searched for his old college notes, and he was proud to share with me an abbreviated cliff notes version of Aquinas' famous book titled, "The Summa in 25 pages" that helped him pass his course. I received it skeptically from Tom not knowing what to expect and, surprisingly, it did help me pass the course.

Not too long ago, Tom discovered that learning about God in terms of rules, dogmas, and conditions was not as important as finding himself growing spiritually with God and understanding that God's mercy was endless. Tom's attitude began to change, a subtle spiritual change. He learned that there are things beyond his control and that God is the only one who could fix them. He began to rely on prayers more so and asked us to pray for his intentions every Monday. When Ursula was scheduled for surgery, he wanted all his friends to be present during the anointing. Vis-a-vie, Tom would never miss being present for anyone's anointing, feeling that his small part in the healing blessing would make a difference. Personally, for Tom, he felt God's healing presence for his son, Sean, who experienced a near-death motorcycle accident, and for Ursula's recent surgeries.

Throughout the past years, when Tom was praying with us, there wasn't a time that Tom hadn't mentioned the love of his life, Ursula, and his children. First and foremost, each Monday, he asked all of us to pray for Ursula whether she was undergoing medical treatment, or for her just to have a good day. As you listened to him speak about Ursula, he spoke with that same young puppy love they had the day they first met. The story got old after two years since he said it often, but Tom's version said that when he laid eyes on her across the campus with her friends, his heart started beating, and he felt he didn't have a chance because she was too beautiful and too smart for him. Using Tom's vernacular, "She was a looker!" We agreed with him jokingly that he married up. I'm sure Ursula has her version as well, but from the eyes of Tom, he would have it no other way. Ursula is and will always be his true love. Gentlemen, we can all learn from Tom how to live a Sacramental marriage in the purest way. Ursula, I sincerely mean this when I say that Tom would like for me to thank you for being the primary instrument in forming him into the person of Christ, for the pursuit of holiness, and for finding true happiness.

Sean, Patrick, Kevin, and Page, clearly it is evident that your family's faith and love is strong, which reflects your parent's love for each other and having Christ in your family. You knew your father better than any of us. Tom's father had passed away early in his life, and he wanted to be a father to you in a way that he didn't have. You all know how much he loved you, and he wasn't shy in telling you so. He felt he should have, could have, done more for all of you to help you find true happiness. We reminded Tom that his views of happiness could be different from yours, but he corrected us by saying that he understood that. But what he prayed for was that you would all find true happiness in the things he discovered about God's Love. When he discovered God's love in all His creation, your father found peace and wanted you to have it as well. What father would not want that for his children? With your father's passing, Tom would like you to know that he is now your Brother in Christ. Pray regularly and, when you pray, talk to him! He will be there for you; he will listen, and he will be your greatest advocate to God for eternity.

For this community, God made Tom Callan for a reason and, as we reflect on our many encounters with Tom, those reasons will quickly be revealed. For me, there are many, but the greatest of all is that Tom Callan taught me that real men CRY! How could you not cry when you learn to love like God?

Tom Callan died on the same day he did his grouping. We never know when God will call us from this earth, but to have an opportunity to group on his last day was a grace for Tom and his friends in the group - which validates the 4th day.

In a fashion typical for Tom, I know he would like to end his Eulogy in a way fitting for a Catholic Marine who loved this Country and his Church so much.

I pledge allegiance to the flag…

MY REFLECTION ____

____

____

Prayer Makes Everything Better
Sarah Ingram

I quit my middle school teaching job at the end of the school year. As the summer passed, I landed another job working at a local publishing company working on the content for college math textbooks. Yes, textbooks still exist. Yes, most of the books are online. And yes, a lot of folks still prefer the real thing over the screen. So yes, we're still in business, and I don't think we're going anywhere any time soon.

My first day on the job, I remember seeing this woman walking in wearing very unprofessional clothes, showing a lot of skin, and looking like she hadn't owned a hairbrush in several years. Turns out, she is our motion graphic designer and videographer-- a real artsy and creative person. I initially was very wary of her because I thought she might not be the right person to hang around-- but my extroverted personality always gets the best of me, and I introduced myself.

That was back in May of 2019. Looking back now, I can't imagine a life where Carrie and I aren't friends. I don't even know who I would be in the office without her. People ask us if we knew each other growing up - and we just chuckle. I must tell you- we're probably a sight to see. We couldn't look or act more differently. Carrie is covered in tattoos and a few piercings and smokes cigarettes regularly. She would call herself a Buddhist, but she doesn't really know anything about Buddha (I've asked). She's very "hippy dippy," as my mother would say. But I will tell you that she has a kind heart, and she is really trying to find peace and love in this world.

About a month into our friendship, Carrie and I started taking 15-minute breaks to go for a walk outside. Initially, these were small talk conversations but, eventually, we started talking about deeper and deeper things. We talked about guys and our dating lives, about how we wished more people would just be empathetic. We talked about how it's strange how folks are so quick to be nice to an animal and even quicker to dismiss the needs of a stranger.

One day Carrie went home for lunch, and I noticed she didn't return at her usual time. I figured she was just taking her dogs for an extra-long walk. At 3 pm, I texted her. No response. At 4 pm, she finally calls me. She says she had a panic attack, blacked out, and crashed into the curb leaving her apartment. She doesn't know how she got back home. All she knows is what the officers told her.

When I was a child, a mentor of mine told me that in crisis situations you don't say, "Can I help at all?" You say, "How can I help?" It puts the emphasis on the actions needed, not your capability. So, I asked Carrie, "How can I help?"

She said, "Do you think you can come over and just sit with me? I'm afraid I'm going to do something and not be aware of it." I left work immediately and sat with her. I took her dogs for a walk while she napped. I even organized her fridge because I got a little bored, truthfully.

The next day I took the day off to pick her up and take her to her psychiatrist. She was given a new prescription. I drove her to the pharmacy, and we waited there together. I bought her lunch, and we ate it outside on the curb at Harris Teeter - no talking, just enjoying the sunshine.Carrie was too scared to go over the bridges, and in Charleston, that's pretty much all we have. We took back roads between all our destinations. I stayed with her as she called her insurance company to handle the bills and her mom to tell her what had been happening.

I want to pause here and emphasize, though, that all these things are just "being a good person." They're not the apostolic action we learned about in the Action rollo. I had made a friend. I was being a friend. But I hadn't yet found a way to bring Carrie to Christ.

I shared my friendship with Carrie at my weekly Cursillo grouping and my sisters encouraged me to keep praying for her and to pray for myself, that I would be aware of the right time to plant seeds. That's what I did- I started intentionally including Carrie's health in my prayers.

A few weeks went by, and Carrie was better, mostly. Then one day it all changed. She again had a panic attack and blacked out. Somehow she ended up parked in the Harris Teeter parking lot, again, not remembering how she got there. She called me, sobbing over the phone, asking if I could come pick her up and take her home. Of course, I did. But THIS time, I would also pray intentionally for her while I drove. And because I knew she was being attacked by so many different demons, I prayed the St. Michael prayer for her, too. As I drove her home and dropped her off, she caught me mumbling under my breath. She asked me what I was saying, and I told her I was praying for her and her health. She thanked me and that was that. Nothing else.

About a week later, I found an image of the St. Michael prayer online and sent it to Carrie with a message. "Hey Carrie. I just want you to know that I've been praying the St. Michael prayer for you with all these attacks that you have been under. In the Catholic faith, we believe that St. Michael is the greatest defender, that he can cast down into Hell Satan and all the evil spirits who attack us humans. I am praying for your protection and I'm praying for your healing. I'm sending along the prayer for you in case you wish to pray it, too." She replied instantly with "Oh my goodness, thank you! This is exactly what I need! I do feel like I'm being attacked, and I know I need some other force to help me, that I can't just "will" these problems away. Thank you so much for praying for me. It really means a lot."

This was in October. Now, most of my talks with Carrie center around God and religion. She still insists on being "Buddhist" but she knows that I pray for her, and she'll even ask me for prayers. We talk about how God is love and that's what the world needs. The world needs Love with a capital L. I tell her about what I learned at Mass, and she tells me what she's learned in her guided meditations. I pray that I exhale Christ so that she may inhale Him. I hope I am inspiring her.

I wouldn't have been able to share these prayers with Carrie if I had not had a strong prayer and study life prior. It would not have meant anything to her if I had not followed the "make a friend, be a friend" method. Carrie trusts me, and I'm slowly working on making her more agreeable to Christianity. I'm trying to bloom, right where I've been planted in a small, college math textbook publishing company. Christ and I are an overwhelming majority and, as long as I keep inviting Him into my relationship with Carrie, He will be there. He will overwhelm us, and He will be the majority of what we focus on. People need people. And, although Carrie might not recognize it now, she needs Christ. I am the Church for her. I just keep praying that I represent our Lord well.

MY REFLECTION ____

____

____

Chapter Twenty

Total Security

Total Security Summary
Tommy Smith

There we were. The last rollo of our weekend. Most of us were exhausted, and ready to go home, but full of joy and The Holy Spirit. We were tired of taking notes, and Mass was just a few minutes away. Yet, one of the most important rollos of the weekend was about to be delivered. Total Security. Properly lived in our 4th Day, it does indeed give us Total Security in keeping our 4th Day vibrant and growing.

We were introduced to Friendship Group Reunion as the cornerstone of living a 4th Day that would keep our journey fresh and growing. Grouping weekly with our brothers and sisters and sharing our weeks with them allows us to be fed as we feed others.

Piety, truly understood, is that one thing during the week that drew our focus to Jesus. It may have been prayer time or Mass or the Rosary or any number of other activities that connected us to Jesus.

Sharing our close moments with Our Lord allowed us to invite others into our unique journeys, as He shed light on His great love for us.

What are we studying to learn more about Our Lord and Savior so that we can become closer to being a mirror image of Him. (I am sure you are saying to yourselves right now, "You cannot love what you do not know.")

What was our apostolic action this past week? How did we attempt to change our environment to Christ? What was our apostolic failure last week? We do not concern ourselves with the emotions of succeeding or failing. Rather, are we taking the gifts God has given us and using them to love our brothers and sisters?

Finally, we look at what our plan is for the coming week and what is the Group doing to change the world to Christ? We learned that this format is a recipe that enlivens our time together and inspires our week's efforts for Our Lord and the Kingdom. We also learned that, if we deviate, we could easily dilute the work of the Holy Spirit.

The last piece of Total Security is Ultreya. Ultreyas were what we experienced at the end of each day when we had testimonies from the team and candidates as well as grouping around the rollo reviews offered by the different tables. Ultreyas continue to feed each Cursillista by drawing all the area group reunions together to continue to allow for deeper friendships as well as encouragement and inspiration for our 4th Day. It is another element to ensuring our 4th Day is vibrant and growing. Ultreyas complement the individual group reunions as a family reunion complements a family. Both are necessary for families to grow and prosper. Ultreyas are also necessary for our Cursillo movement to grow and prosper.

And… there it was – Total Security – total acknowledgment of His power and presence in our lives as we gather weekly and monthly to share that power and presence and to glorify His name!

MY REFLECTION ____

____

____

My "Road to Emmaus" Experience
Dennis Mahoney

It has been over ten years since I lived my Cursillo weekend in 2013. I've been married to my wife "Saint Nancy" for almost 55 years now, and we have five wonderful, married children, with 11 grandchildren. As background, I am also a cradle Catholic. I went to a Catholic grade school and, while there, seriously considered becoming a priest. While my vocation changed, I have been very active in the Church since my days as an altar boy, choir member, Lector, Eucharistic Minister, CCD teacher, and Parish Council member. I have also held leadership positions in the Knights of Columbus. Since I was raised on the Baltimore Catechism, I always knew why God made us…to Know Him, Love Him, and Serve Him in this world… to be happy with Him for eternity in Heaven.

While my faith has always been important to me, while I wa growing up my view of our faith was all about ME getting to Heaven… following the rules. So, when I came to my Cursillo weekend, I thought "I'm a good practicing Catholic, and this will be a nice retreat"…and since I hadn't been on one in years, maybe it would help me get closer to God. While open to the workings of the Spirit, I thought I already had the Piety (Love Him) and Study (Know Him) down, and certainly I had spent my whole life in serving Him (my definition of Action) but seeing God in others (*all created in the image & likeness of God*) and demonstrating God's love and sharing my faith (Apostolic Action/ Evangelizing) just wasn't my thing.

You see, I'm also an engineer, very analytical. Some might say cold or aloof. My relationship with God was more "*Old Testament,*" more "follow the rules, fear the Lord," than seeing God as "Love." In fact, looking back, I don't remember any emphasis, or ever learning or feeling that God loved me. (Maybe it's just that I'm old now and my memory has failed me.) My faith was all about obedience to an all-powerful God, with having a strong sense of duty and, again, about working on me getting to Heaven.

That changed for me on my weekend while I was sitting at one of those tables. I had been, listening to the talks and participating in the discussions, but waiting for the bolt of lightning that struck St. Paul to hit me, waiting to hear God speaking clearly to me and telling me what

I needed to do. During one of the Rollos (*Christianity in Action*), while the speaker was relating his Christian outreach to a person in need, I had that "Road to Emmaus" experience that the two disciples had walking with Jesus after his Resurrection – and my heart was burning…and it all clicked. It was finally the "Bolt of Lightning" I had been waiting for, like the words of the Prophet Ezekiel 36:26 *("I will give you a new heart, and a new spirit I will put within you. I will remove the heart of stone from your flesh and give you a heart of flesh.")*. I felt the warm glow of God's love, and I finally understood that I needed to care about and share Him with others.

So, what did I do?   Well, after that weekend mountain-top experience, I joined a weekly reunion group that meets to talk about our journey to God in terms of our 3-legged stool of Piety, Study and Apostolic Action. During those meetings, one of our group members talked about his involvement in the Kairos Prison Ministries, which is a non-denominational Cursillo for those who are in Prison. Not necessarily the first group of individuals I would have picked to bring Christ's love to…but visiting those in prison is one of the Corporal Works of Mercy. My friend invited me to get involved, and I participated in a weekend "walk" at Allendale Correctional Institution as a table servant. What a "Washing of the Feet" service experience that was! What I experienced both in my Cursillo weekend, in my weekly group reunions, and especially in the Kairos weekend was first-hand experience of the love of God in Action, of bringing that love to others - and I was a part of it! The change in men that I have seen as a team member on many Cursillo weekends has been amazing, but the change in the men in that prison from the time we first met with them on Thursday evening (and you thought you were suspicious on your Weekend!) to the sharing that they had in the open mic session on Saturday night was nothing short of miraculous! To listen to grown men in tears regretting their choices but, more than that, recognizing the love of God that they had experienced through the talks, and especially in the interactions with the Kairos volunteers and their fellow inmates was the most moving experience I have ever had.

While I feel good about this, I recognize that we are all on a pilgrimage to God, and that while each one of us has some calling, we are merely tools that God is using to knock on the door of the hearts of men and women around us. I've been fortunate to have seen many individuals opening that door to let Him in. As Catholic Christians, this is what it means to Know, Love & Serve Him, to be part of the Mystical Body of Christ. To quote St. Theresa of Avila: *"He has no hands, no feet on earth but yours. Yours are the eyes through which he looks compassion on this world. Yours are the feet with which he walks to do good."*

Then I heard the voice of the Lord, saying, "Whom shall I send, and who will go for Us?" Then I said, "Here am I. Send me!" Isaiah 6:8
"As the Father has sent me, so I send you" Jn. 20:21.

MY REFLECTION ____

____

____

Living With Joy
Martin Ramirez.

I am originally from a town near Córdoba Veracruz, Mexico. I lived my Cursillo from July 24 to 27, 2008, course number 100 in the Diocese of Raleigh, North Carolina. From that date, I began to live my fourth day, a fourth day that has not been easy given the circumstances and the fact of being a person with defects, which include my sins and spirituality. But I also have virtues, virtues that, little by little, I have been improving for personal, social, and ecclesial good.

After living the course, when I look at my past, I realize that Our Lord fulfills His Word and His promises in each one of those who make the decision to follow and love him. I am a faithful witness because in this time that has elapsed in my fourth day, it has been more by His Grace and Love that I still stand. Without God's Grace, we cannot stand and be good Christians, as we are living in sin before living a Cursillo. Many times we make decisions without consulting Him in prayer, and we fail in our plans because it is Our Lord that we must invite to be with us since He is and He said in His Word, "I will be with you until the end of time."

When we make decisions without God, we often realize those decisions may adversely affect our spiritual life. Still, He is always there with us and for us. Having a child is not a bad thing, but having my son with the woman I did, I realized it was not the right thing to do. I was not thinking about how she was living her life, and this bothers me because I didn't include God. My conscience still bothers me. I think, though, that God is pushing me through this by allowing me to live my life the way He wants me to, and to ensure that I give my son everything he needs. including knowing God.

On this pilgrimage path, I have learned to help the one who has fallen without any reckless judgment, but rather to reach out to him to lift him up and be that friend he needs. When one puts himself in the shoes of the other or has suffered something similar, you recognize that we all need the other to walk and thus sustain us in this battle against the enemy. I have learned to understand those who cry and suffer. I have learned to be more helpful and tolerant with the little ones.

Thanks to the course, I could heal wounds of the past that hurt me and did not let me be full and happy. Childhood traumas discouraged me, and I did not know how to overcome them. I was a person with a grudge towards some members of my family for the absence of any of them in my childhood. I made mistakes that damaged me, and I did not know how to make amends for them. Thank God I lived the Cursillo! All those black clouds dissipated, and I could see the solution to those evils that afflicted me. I learned to forgive, to make amends for the wrong I had done, and to forgive myself for the bad decisions I made before the course. As we say, I began to see life "in colors."

Therefore, I want to continue living until God calls me to His presence with the help of my Cursillo brothers and the prayers of all. I hope one day to enjoy what Our Lord promises us in His Word, to enjoy eternal life, and to reach my fifth day with joy and without fear. I long to hear the words of Christ telling me, "Come, blessed, to my Father and take possession of what belongs to you." When I read those words, I am filled with encouragement and joy. I know this is my hope, but I recognize that to deserve it, I must continue to fulfill God's mission for me. I have done so and will continue to do so until I can achieve the reward of eternal life with Him. With the joy of knowing that God loves me, I continue to live my fourth day with hope and renewal. Day by day, I do His bidding, hoping to please Him, and waiting to be forever with Him.

Pray for me. I will pray for you. God bless you. De Colores!

MY REFLECTION ____

____

____

Living in Total Security
Kristin Creed

I made my Cursillo weekend in March of 2008 at Our Lady of the Hills Catholic Church. It was the women's weekend #52 in South Carolina. I was a "cradle Catholic," always considered myself faithful, and was involved in parish life. My weekend, however, opened my eyes in a whole new way! One of the phrases that resonated with me the most was, "You and God are an overwhelming majority." Here is one example of how living out my Fourth Day faithfully and trusting in Jesus has blessed me and so many others as I continue to see the outpouring of the Holy Spirit at work in Our Lady of Peace parish.

I was asked by Fr. Sandy McDonald several years before making my Cursillo weekend to "lead" the Evangelization ministry at our parish. I really didn't know what to do, and so all I did was stand by a poster in the Narthex each fall during our ministry fair. After making my weekend, I felt led by the Holy Sprit to do something different. Many journal entries speak of my struggles and insecurity about actually leading something, and I wondered about turning things over to someone who was "truly" a leader.

I had an opportunity in early 2009 to speak before the parish. Our Deacon said we were not going to do the typical ministry fair and instead ministry leaders were going to speak from the ambo inviting people to join their ministry. Though I was looking to turn things over to someone new, as a lector I did not mind speaking in front of the parish, so I took the next step and spoke after the masses one weekend. (As a side note—I believe myself and maybe one other were the only ministry leaders to speak at that time….)

I prayed during my adoration hour each week and wrote my appeal. After speaking at mass I had about 10 people sign up! I set up a meeting and that was the beginning of monthly meetings for about the next 10 years in which we began and ended in prayer, asking for the guidance of the Holy Spirit. Here is what I wrote in my journal after the first meeting: "…the energy of that group was absolutely amazing!…I literally felt the Spirit in that place! Awesome.

When you let go and let God it ALWAYS works out PERFECTLY! He knows what He's doing!" Over the years, that team mainly focused on parish enrichment, believing that our parishioners were our best resource to evangelize others. We were responsible for the biannual parish mission; we coordinated Newcomer Welcome events; we bought Matthew Kelly books for our parish each Christmas, and the "Little" books for parishioners each Liturgical Season. We were responsible for the message on our parish sign plus many other activities to reach out to different groups within the parish, including our Hispanic Community and School.

Looking back now, one thing that amazes me is the fact that almost every person involved in that ministry is now a Cursillista! I see the impact they each have had on their environments, and I am in awe of how the Holy Spirit has been at work: leaders in RCIA, visiting the sick and bringing Eucharist to the homebound, a new rosary makers ministry, "far away" friends and family brought to the Catholic faith. I have invited them all to share their own stories and I hope and pray they will. I see how Jesus always answers my prayers in the best possible way (even, and maybe especially when it is not MY way). He continues to send the Holy Spirit to work among us. I am so excited and it truly gives me hope. I had to overcome fears and insecurities (and of course I still struggle with this), but once I truly embraced the fact that Jesus is always with me and if I trust and follow His will, He will provide and multiply my meager gifts, I wasblessed 100-fold with the grace to see the Holy Spirit at work! God is the One and only true leader." We are simply His humble servants. Be not afraid. De Colores!

MY REFLECTION ____

____

____

Conclusion

Okay, you have reached the end of the book. What now? Do you put the book on your bookshelf and move on? Do you say that was wonderful and remark to yourself how interesting the testimonies were? Do you pick up the phone and ask our Bishop what he thought of the book? Do you talk to your small group and get their opinions? I suspect you might do all these things. But I have a better idea.

This book was written to encourage, inspire, and give guidance for our 4th day journey. The weekend was a prelude to the rest of our lives. It was a prelude to the rest of our lives living connected to Jesus Christ. It was a prelude to making the most of our lives for Jesus and his Kingdom. We were chosen, and yes each one of us was chosen by the Holy Spirit to go and share the gospel and live our lives in such a way that the world will change back to Jesus Christ. The book is meant to remind us of that grand weekend and how life can be if we stay connected to Jesus.: "I AM THE VINE. YOU ARE THE BRANCHES. WHOEVER REMAINS IN ME AND I IN HIM WILL BEAR MUCH FRUIT BECAUSE WITHOUT ME YOU CAN DO NOTHING." JOHN 15:5.

We can do NOTHING without Him. But we can do all things with Him. So, use this book to remind you of what we are asked to do for Him. Draw constant encouragement from it. Draw constant inspiration from it. Draw constant guidance and therefore energy from it. Let's go and change the world for Christ by changing one person at a time to Him. Let's start with us. And that is why this book was written. For you.

DeColores,
Tommy Smith